SNMP Mastery

Michael W Lucas

Tilted
Windmill
Press

Copyright Information

SNMP Mastery

Michael W Lucas

More Tech Books from Michael W Lucas

Absolute BSD

Absolute OpenBSD (1st and 2nd edition)

Cisco Routers for the Desperate (1st and 2nd edition)

PGP and GPG

Absolute FreeBSD (2nd and 3rd edition)

Network Flow Analysis

the IT Mastery Series

SSH Mastery (1st and 2nd edition)

DNSSEC Mastery

Sudo Mastery (1st and 2nd edition)

FreeBSD Mastery: Storage Essentials

Networking for Systems Administrators

Tarsnap Mastery

FreeBSD Mastery: ZFS

FreeBSD Mastery: Specialty Filesystems

FreeBSD Mastery: Advanced ZFS

PAM Mastery

Relayd and Httpd Mastery

Ed Mastery

FreeBSD Mastery: Jails

Novels (as Michael Warren Lucas)

Immortal Clay

Kipuka Blues

Butterfly Stomp Waltz

Terrapin Sky Tango

Hydrogen Sleets

git commit murder

Brief Contents

Complete Contents

Acknowledgements

Writing a book on SNMP feels like reconstructing a culture five millennia gone. All you can do is scavenge and rebuild all the busted-up bits of clay tablets it left behind. It's possible, but deciphering cuneiform that varies by region and century will give you such a headache. The reasons for many design decisions are lost in thirty-year-old unindexed mailing lists, and many of the perpetrators have passed. Additionally, everybody's experience with SNMP differs, and everyone has implemented SNMP slightly differently.

This means my technical reviewers were more important than in any other book I've written. I sincerely thank James Allen, Tim Enders, Ilya Etingof, John-Mark Gurney, Pieter Hollants, Joni Julian, Johannes Kastl, John Liggett, JP Mens, Florian Obser, Mike O'Connor, Shawn O'Shea, Gavin Rebeiro, Neil Roza, and Adam Thompson for providing the breadth of experience with this most pervasive and perplexing of protocols. I must especially thank Martijn van Duren, for helping me understand SNMP to a degree that can't possibly be healthy.

Why would I write a book on SNMP? Well, Kurt Mosiejczuk says, "Really, I blame myself." To which all I can say is:

Good. He should. *I* certainly do.

Chapter 0: Introduction

The Simple Network Management Protocol, *SNMP*, seemed like a great idea at the time. Computer vendors needed a straightforward protocol that allowed devices to communicate management information to one another. System managers should be able to sit at a central console and command their entire fleet: start that process, close that interface, kick that user off the system, acknowledge that error, dispatch that intern for coffee, blackhole that spammer, and so on. Such a protocol should be both straightforward and highly structured. Everyone came to an agreement on the requirements and how the protocol should work, and thus was spawned SNMP.

Then the real world got involved, with predictably disastrous results.

Some developers and organizations went all-in on SNMP, determined that their product should be a first-class network citizen. Others added bare-bones SNMP as an afterthought, or only in response to customer demand. Equipment evolved in ways that SNMP's creators didn't anticipate, and vendor engineering teams either thoughtfully stretched the standard to fit reality or slapped something together and went for a drink.

Thirty-odd years later, SNMP's simplicity has suffered indignities best not discussed in polite company. Some folks have attempted to create more "modern" network management protocols, but those efforts offered no real improvement over SNMP, haven't achieved wide adoption, or both. Some vendors have implemented proprietary protocols, which work tremendously well so long as you use only that vendor's equipment.

SNMP takes a lot of heat for complexity. "It has *simple* right in the name, but produces all these long streams of numbers and weird abbreviations? *Please!*" The protocol underlying SNMP itself is not at all complex, but it blatantly exposes our digital infrastructure's ever-swelling complexity. Additionally, some organizations implemented SNMP software and libraries so poorly and insecurely that they've soiled the protocol's reputation.

We're left with a protocol that's incredibly powerful and flexible, but bears all the scars of its history. SNMP lets you invoke ancient standards from the void. It grants you incredible system-changing power, and can destroy everything you've worked for. SNMP exposes the secrets of your servers, and—if you're thoughtless—reconfigures them into unspeakable nightmares. It's like something out of an H. P. Lovecraft tale, without the rampant xenophobia but with all the alien system topologies.[1] Just call this book *The Networknomicon*.

SNMP is network duct tape. It works on both servers and network hardware alike. It works on Unix and Linux and Windows. While TCP/IP and UDP are the common protocols, vendors of old implemented support for IPX and AppleTalk and CLNS and whatever protocol made sense for their equipment. SNMP runs on otherwise wildly incompatible devices that no rational person would consider interconnecting, which is good because most medium-to-large networks contain a distressingly large number of devices that no rational person would consider interconnecting. Like SNMP itself, installing every one of them made sense at the time.

SNMP doesn't produce pretty graphs or reports. It generates data that you feed to other tools that generate pretty graphs and nicely formatted reports. Some tools hide their SNMP underpinnings behind friendly interfaces. But when the pretty GUI doesn't have the feature you want or flat-out fails, you must dig into the protocol underneath.

Basic SNMP gives you unprecedented ability to extract data from hosts. Mastering SNMP lets you issue commands to remote hosts. It's not that SNMP is the be-all and end-all of systems and network management, but SNMP can offer solutions when nothing else works.

---

[1] The topologies were there all along. Your shallow human mind was blissfully incapable of perceiving them.

This whole analogy is disturbingly apropos.

System Components

SNMP uses the standard client-server model, but it's a little different from management protocols like Secure Shell (SSH). An individual SNMP query can be sent and answered before an SSH session finishes negotiating connection parameters.

An SNMP *manager* is the client software that issues SNMP requests. It's called a manager because it's expected to extract management information from devices and issue commands to them.

An SNMP *agent* is the server running on a device such as a router, server, or workstation. An agent is a little more dynamic than most server software; it's expected to be able to interrogate the local system and provide information to the manager, and it might even reconfigure the host if it's configured properly. A human agent performs work for you, supposedly according to your wishes. An SNMP agent also labors at your command, but on a remote host—and theoretically adheres more closely to your desires than any human agent.

A *network management system*, or *NMS*, is a manager that's designed to collect data and issue commands to agents. It probably also runs tools for managing systems via several other protocols. It includes programs that transform SNMP and other data into pretty human-readable graphs so you can make decisions.

I'll also occasionally refer to *monitoring systems*. This is a server or software that runs SNMP queries and transforms the data into human-friendly graphs and charts and tables, and/or sends alerts when something breaks. It's different than an NMS in that it only requires read access to your agents; that's why I differentiate it from a full-on NMS. If you're running Cacti, MRTG, Graphite, or one of their competitors, it's a monitoring system. Zabbix, Nagios, and Icinga have some NMS features. OpenNMS and HP BTO/OpenView are examples of full-featured NMSes.[2]

---

2   The plural of NMS is not "nemesis." Unfortunately.

How SNMP is Used

Organizations use SNMP for some sort of monitoring and some variety of discovery. A few also use it to issue commands to remote devices.

In routine operation, a network management system acts as an SNMP *manager*. The manager sends a query across the network to an agent, and accepts values in return. The manager processes these answers, probably either storing or alerting on them. The manager might also accept unsolicited informational messages (*traps*) from agents. The manager doesn't need any friendly human-facing tools, describing what it wants: it simply spits a number at an agent and accepts the answer. That number might look lengthy to humans, but it's trivial to the machines.

Discovery is wholly different, because humans are involved.

All those numbers that the monitoring system queries? Someone has to figure out what to monitor. Monitoring is among the blackest of sysadmin arts, and is highly dependent on the organization's resources, management organization, and technical talent. Some management systems automatically recognize certain agents and select a few default characteristics. Everybody and their pet ghast automatically monitors network bandwidth usage. But even the best management systems can't automatically know what you care about. Each organization has its own definition of *useful*.

This means that in addition to the raw numbers used by SNMP-based monitoring, the manager must also support a human-friendly[3] interface. It should be able to describe what the various numbers mean, and offer some guidance on how to interpret them.

This book offers guidance on both types of usage, but spends more pages on the more complicated human-facing usage. "Run this query and accept a number" is very straightforward… once you know which query to run.

---

3   For some value of "human-friendly."

Where SNMP Goes Wrong

If this is all SNMP is, why do some many people gripe about it? The Management Information Base looks complex, but it's not that hard once you understand how it arranges information. The command line looks baroque, but if you read the manual for grep(1) you'll see SNMP commands are no worse than other Unix suites.

SNMP went wrong when people started implementing it. The protocol is pretty simple. The standards documents seem clear, but leave room for interpretation. Vendors interpreted any vagueness in ways that suited their goals and biases. Some thoughtfully implemented features in a way they thought would best suit the customer. Some of those vendors had no idea how their customers used their products or how real people used SNMP. Others chose to implement the standard in the fastest, easiest way possible. Still others thought the standard was poorly considered, and instead implemented something almost but not quite like the standard. While many vendors use the freely available net-snmp toolkit (formerly known as ucd-snmp) as their base implementation, others wrote their own or licensed a commercial implementation. Every one of them changed the software in ways they thought sensible.

SNMP is clean and easy. SNMP implementations are all unique. Some are more unique than others. The only way to learn your vendor's biases is to play with their product. This, right here, is why people curse SNMP.

Learning a protocol, and simultaneously learning your vendor's abuses of that protocol, is nightmarish. That's why this book exists, so you can understand the protocol before learning your vendor's software.

Always remember that many different organizations implemented SNMP. Not all implemented it correctly. Many made different design decisions. Some made unique design decisions, or violated the standard to fit their goals or resources. The biggest headache of SNMP is understanding exactly what your vendor did.

Performance

One common complaint people have with SNMP is that it places a heavy load on the manager. The problem here isn't with SNMP, but in how it's deployed.

The first time you tell an agent to dump everything it knows, even on a small host, you'll discover stuff you never thought existed. Under standard SNMP, you can pull twenty-two characteristics from every network interface. Many of these can be graphed or monitored. The obvious choices are inbound and outbound traffic. Everybody wants to know how much traffic their hosts exchange. Then you might want to make sure that your network interfaces all run at consistent speeds, rather than flapping around in a miasma of autonegotiation. Yep, there's an SNMP object for that. There's this thing called "unknown protocols" that sounds like it'd be a useful indicator of network issues, so we'll monitor that. Without serious restraint, you'll find yourself monitoring a dozen intriguing values.

Then there's disk storage. You can monitor how full partitions are, how much virtual memory is used (which isn't really a disk but it makes sense that it might be reported as such), and how many storage allocation failures each has had. You probably don't graph the storage device block size, but all the other stuff looks quite useful to a sysadmin.

Add in the size of the queue of delayed email, the installed software, the daemons running, and every other aspect of the host. To a sysadmin, this is all really cool stuff that you don't normally get to watch. So you go into your nifty monitoring system and tell it to graph a hundred and fifty different things on your server. It works! SNMP grants you a degree of visibility you have never before experienced, allowing you to transcend the merely mortal and peer into the workings of the greater universe.

Then you deploy that template against your fleet of servers, routers, switches, and virtual machines… and your monitoring system bogs down.

A single SNMP query is quick and easy. A hundred and fifty of them every minute against one agent are fine. Repeat that against a hundred agents, though, and you have fifteen thousand queries a minute. This means your management host handles 250 SNMP queries a second. The flood of esoteric knowledge will absolutely crush a minimal-spec virtual machine, like Cthulhu showing up at the neighborhood coffee shop, ordering an extra-large latte with all the foam, and plopping down in a chair with his laptop.

Set the SNMP processes aside for a moment. A management host almost always runs a monitoring system. That system might or might not query efficiently. Some of those systems still use primordial query methods that were obsoleted twenty-five years ago. Worse, the system might not store data efficiently. An SNMP query that returns quickly can appear to back up the system if your monitoring system saturates the disk with writes.

Once you understand SNMP, you'll spend the rest of your career learning what to use it *for*. I'll make occasional recommendations, but what you should monitor depends entirely on your goals, your network, and your hosts. My one evergreen recommendation is you should always monitor the amount of network traffic used by your management host. Monitoring traffic should comprise a tiny part of your overall network traffic.[4]

Security

People joke that SNMP stands for "Security? Not My Problem!" Others are completely serious about saying it. It runs over UDP, so there's not even a guarantee of message delivery. None of that is accurate, except when it is.

The first versions of SNMP date from 1988. SNMP was designed based on experience with Simple Gateway Monitoring Protocol (SGMP), and was intended as an interim protocol until something

---

4   I have successfully saturated a gigabit Ethernet connection with overaggressive monitoring. I have faith that you can too!

better came along. The Internet was a United-States-centric entity, with very limited presence in other nations. Internet access meant you were at a university, in the military, or worked for a defense contractor. Supercomputers of the day had less processor power than today's shabbiest cellphone, and time on those processors was billed to individual departments. Primordial SNMP transmitted everything in clear text, exactly like everything else.

The earliest SNMP implementations provided access control via a *community string*, a text string that provided access to the agent. There's a long argument about why a community string is not technically a password, but it's irrelevant. A community string is a password that grants access to the SNMP agent.

Today's Internet is completely different. Nations actively engaged in shooting wars with one another share access to the Internet. Transport-layer encryption is almost universal. If you use old SNMP versions over today's Internet, you deserve to have a script kiddie mess with your systems. Modern SNMP is encrypted. The encryption isn't as strong as that used for SSH or HTTPS, but an intruder without a username and password must do a whole bunch of work to crack your traffic.

SNMP differentiates between read-only access and read-write access. Different communities and usernames have different access levels, or perhaps even access to different subsets of information. Your monitoring system should have read-only access to agents. Instructing an agent to change the system, such as altering a configuration file, restarting a daemon, or rebooting the whole host, requires read-write access and supporting software.

SNMP agents are supposed to provide information on the host they run on. They also can issue commands to the host, provided that have the privileges to do so—generally, `root` access, or carefully carved out exceptions in policy-based security. This means you must run a well-programmed, well-secured SNMP agent.

Many early SNMP agents shipped with two default communities enabled, `public` and `private`. They've been considered security risks for more than three decades. If you find either of these communities enabled on any agent, disable them and feed your predecessor to the unspeakable entities powering your network.

SNMP Software

We'll learn SNMP with the industry-standard net-snmp toolkit (http://www.net-snmp.org) available for Windows and every modern Unix. Set up a small Unix virtual machine for experimenting with net-snmp. Other programs have prettier pointy-clicky interfaces, yes. But a major purpose of SNMP is to produce data to feed to other tools, and command-line tools best fit that task. The various net-snmp tools behave the way they do because they're designed in accordance with SNMP, so we'll dive into *why* the tools work as well as merely *how*. Net-snmp is also extensible, allowing you to do customized reporting on your applications and systems.

Device vendors often use net-snmp as the basis for their agents. Many write their own, or license and modify a commercial agent. In some devices, there's no way to tell where the agent originated. This book talks a bunch about configuring net-snmp, because everyone *can* get it.

Windows deprecated its default SNMP agent in 2012. You can still install it, but it's a peasant in the Windows ecosystem. Many organizations provide Windows SNMP agents, and you can use net-snmp's agent on Windows. Once you understand SNMP, configuring any Windows SNMP agent is trivial. If you have a Windows desktop, install net-snmp for the command line management tools usable via PowerShell.

People new to SNMP will probably want an SNMP browser for their desktop. If you use a Unix workstation, the tkmib graphic browser included in net-snmp is the standard. Tkmib takes all of its configuration from net-snmp, letting you easily replicate your exact command line in graphic form. SnmpB is a solid, free Windows MIB browser.

I will not cover any user-facing data processing tools. People feed SNMP data to tools like Icinga and MRTG and Cacti and Graphite and dozens more. I've used bunches of them. The only things these tools have in common is that they eat SNMP and excrete data in a manner the organization finds useful. Each organization has different needs, so I cannot legitimately declare that any of them is the One True Eater Of SNMP.

No, wait—these friendly-looking tools all have one other thing in common. It's something that they share with all software.

They break when fed unexpected data.

And when they break, you must dig into the underlying SNMP queries and responses to understand the problem.

That's probably why you're reading this book.

SNMP and Vendors

Many organizations and companies have implemented SNMP in their proprietary gear and provide thick tomes about configuring their specific variant. I can't realistically discuss the specifics of any embedded vendor. I will, however, give you the context so that you can configure these devices to behave the way you want. If a tutorial from your vendor tells you how to configure a community string, for example, you'll know that it's referring to unencrypted and unauthenticated communications via SNMPv2c or even SNMPv1. Deciphering the vendor's configuration syntax and simultaneously learning a protocol is not impossible; it's merely impossible to do correctly.

Every vendor can choose its own, slightly different default settings for different parts of the SNMP protocol. While I walk you through examples using net-snmp, the real key is understanding the context of those examples. We'll discuss features like authentication and privacy encryption methods, so that you know they exist and what they're used for. That way, when a random agent and a different but equally random manager spews up an error like "unrecognized privacy encryption method," you have some awareness of what that means.

If neither you nor your vendors use net-snmp, many specific examples are of limited utility to you. Focus on the theory and principles presented rather than actual configuration file entries. Your vendor buries similar features somewhere in their configuration. Many of these agents behave similarly to net-snmp in unexpected ways. Many embedded devices must restart their SNMP software to make changes take effect, just as net-snmp's daemons do.

If possible, get a couple pieces of test equipment that match your environment and set up SNMP on them as you go through this book. Create virtual machines that mimic your production hosts. Seize that spare router. When we discuss users, set up users on your net-snmp host and then on those test systems. Run queries against your net-snmp host, then try the same query against your test gear. Explore how *your* devices use SNMP, and how *your* vendors abuse the protocol.

About This Book

Most of my technology books are written with an eye towards an end product. If you read a book about SSH or sudo, you should be able to use the tools securely and configure them to behave the way you want. You finish with a skill set that lets you solidly address a particular problem.

This book is a little different.

SNMP is middleware. It doesn't create graphs, but it produces data to feed to a graph generator. It doesn't set alarm levels (with rare exceptions); it generates data that other software uses to decide if it's going to alarm or not. This book is a component in helping you produce an end product, but it's not an end in and of itself.

Many books conflate the problems of "generate data for monitoring" with "configure the monitoring tool." This book deliberately separates the two. Understanding SNMP before you dig into monitoring and management will ease the whole process of watching your network. You will understand what SNMP can and cannot do, helping you decide if your monitoring suite is doing the best it can or if it's just really bad software.

Who Should Read This Book?

This book is for sysadmins and network administrators who want to extract information from hosts and devices. Your management station can be Unix or Windows, but in either case we'll be spending a lot of time at the command line.

While developers who want to program applications will find this book useful for introducing SNMP's usage and concepts, it contains very little programming information. I would encourage developers to understand something about the user's experience of SNMP before attempting to write an SNMP interface, however.

Learning Prerequisites

Net-snmp has a distinct Unix bias. You'll get the best results if you install a Unix, even as a virtual machine on your laptop.

I used CentOS, Debian, and FreeBSD as my reference platforms. The more closely your Unix resembles one of these, the easier time you'll have. If you run a less common Unix, presumably you're familiar with its funny little ways.

You should know how to search your Unix's package repositories for any programs mentioned. Unix vendors habitually reorganize their package collections the moment I release a book, so I don't list very many packages. I assume you know how and when to escalate your privilege via su, sudo, doas, or whatever your host uses. I don't go into many details on individual Unixes, because they change frequently enough they'd quickly become obsolete. Your Unix might preconfigure examples in this book, or deliberately disable them. Speaking of which...

Debian Issues

Debian and derived Unixes, like Ubuntu, consider the standard SNMP information (MIB) files shipped with net-snmp insufficiently free, and does not include them in their net-snmp package. To realistically learn SNMP on Debian, you must enable the non-free repository and install the snmp-mibs-downloader package on your manager. This installs the MIB files and some other important packages. (As I write this, you'll also need the snmp, snmpd, and libsnmp-dev packages.)

Installing the MIB files is not enough, though: Debian disables reading them. Go to `/etc/snmp/snmp.conf` and comment out the *mibs* keyword. You can now use the tools like everybody else.

What's In This Book?

Chapter 0 is this introduction.

Chapter 1, *SNMP Essentials*, discusses the core elements of SNMP. We'll discuss the core components and how they fit together. We'll also cover some basics about our reference implementation of SNMP, the net-snmp suite.

Chapter 2, *Authentication*, discusses how to authenticate to an SNMP agent. We'll focus on SNMPv3 with its strong authentication and privacy protections, but also cover the simpler communities of older versions.

Chapter 3, *Queries*, covers using manager software to interrogate an agent in a variety of ways.

Chapter 4, *The Management Information Base*, takes you through the details of the MIB, how it's arranged, and how to gather and evaluate MIB files.

Chapter 5, *The Net-SNMP Agent*, discusses configuring and managing the snmpd(8) agent.

Chapter 6, *Logging*, tells you how to manage where net-snmp programs send their errors. Net-snmp takes full advantage of Unix's features in a way many other programs don't bother with.

Chapter 7, *SET*, shows how to change remote systems with SNMP commands.

Chapter 8, *Proxies, SMUX, and AgentX* discusses making an SNMP agent interoperate with other agents and sub-agents.

Chapter 9, *Access Control*, covers restricting users and communities to select parts of the agent.

Chapter 10, *Extending snmpd(8)*, gives you tools to provide customized information via SNMP. This powerful feature lets you take arbitrary details from your operating system and applications and make them available via SNMP.

Chapter 11, *Monitoring*, offers advice on how to monitor critical system components like memory, disk usage, and so on.

Chapter 12, *Traps*, turns SNMP around and lets managers receive messages from agents.

Once you know all this, you'll be able to make any monitoring system dance. Or cry, as appropriate.

Chapter 1: SNMP Essentials

Before we delve into the details of configuring managers and agents, you must understand a few basics about the SNMP protocol. SNMP provides information via a Management Information Base (MIB), which includes a vast assortment of objects indexed by Object Identifiers (OIDs). Learning a bit about them will help you understand your queries.

SNMP can be carried across the network in a variety of methods. We'll briefly discuss those channels and the advantages and disadvantages of each.

Finally, net-snmp has a highly flexible method for handling configuration files. We'll talk about that system and how a new user can best cope with it.

As you're learning SNMP and want to explore different options, look and see if someone has made an agent public. Over at `demo.snmplabs.com` you'll find a nice simulation of Linux and Windows, and router-type agents, with a variety of authentication options and features. There are others, look around.

First, though, the protocol versions.

Variants and Versions

SNMP has undergone many revisions. Some of these revisions never achieved wide adoption, or arrived with fanfare and disappeared silently. We're not going to deal with varieties like SNMPv2 (no "c") or SNMPv2u, SNMP over IPX, or over AppleTalk, or any of the other transports. We will focus on SNMP over TCP/IP, primarily via UDP, as used on the Internet and modern corporate networks.

SNMP version 3 (SNMPv3) is the current protocol. It's extensible, encrypted, and flexible. Released in 2002, all responsible vendors support it. Its flexible authentication system makes possible protocol variations like SNMP over TLS and SNMP over SSH.

SNMP version 2 with community support (SNMPv2c) is the next earlier version. It's unencrypted and runs only over UDP. If your device doesn't support SNMPv3, you're stuck with SNMPv2c. When using SNMPv2c over a shared, public, or otherwise untrusted network, use additional transport-layer security such as a VPN between the manager and your agents.

Both SNMPv2c and SNMPv3 organize queries identically. SNMPv3's improvements are integrated with that format, but the data exchange is identical. If you give your packet sniffer the authentication information needed to decrypt an SNMPv3 query, and compare the results to an SNMPv2c query, they'll look identical.

SNMP version 1 (SNMPv1) is the lowest common denominator. It doesn't support bulk queries, reducing its efficiency, and transmits everything unencrypted. Don't use it unless you have absolutely no other choice. I would prefer skipping it in this book, but a few vendors still ship equipment that only understands SNMPv1. Its underlying query format differs from SNMPv2c and SNMPv3.

The Management Information Base

SNMP organizes information hierarchically, arranging everything by category and sub-category and so on. The definition of this tree is called a *Management Information Base*, or *MIB*. (It's pronounced "mib," not M. I. B.) An individual entry in the Management Information Base is called an *object*. Most objects have a *value*. Each object has a place within the MIB. An *Object Identifier*, or *OID*, is the object's address within the MIB. SNMP software can translate addresses into objects and interpret the value of objects.

Before starting with SNMP you must have a grip of MIBs, objects, and OIDs. People often use all of these words interchangeably. Don't let those people confuse you; these are all distinct and separate entities, and you must comprehend the differences to really understand SNMP. Think of a dashboard. A MIB is the whole dashboard, and a train has a very different dashboard than a rocket. An object might be the speedometer. The object's value is something like "250 kilometers per hour." The OID says "second from the left, on the top row of the dashboard."

A MIB provides definitions for what the objects refer to. SNMP supports many different but interrelated MIBs. MIB names are generally in all caps, except when the authors are trying to communicate something through the name. There's a MIB for general host information under SNMPv2c, SNMPv2-MIB. The MIB HOST-RESOURCES-MIB contains a bunch of stuff for servers and workstations, such as memory and processes and printer errors. There's a MIB for network interfaces (IF-MIB), IP and ICMP traffic (IP-MIB). Organizations can request their own chunk of OID space and issue their own MIBs for their equipment. Each MIB is defined in a text file, usually named after the MIB but with .txt, .mib, or .my at the end—that is, SNMPv2-MIB is defined in SNMPv2-MIB.txt.

SNMP MIBs are written in a structured format called the *Structure of Management Information*, or *SMI*. We currently use SMI version 2, or *SMI-2*. The SMI format requires defining exactly what data you're presenting, and how it's presented. SMI is a slightly tweaked subset of Abstract Syntax Notation version 1 (ASN.1).[5] Phone, manufacturing, power, and other complex interconnected systems use ASN.1, and many use SMI-2.

SMI structures data as a tree. Each entry on the tree, and its children, can contain only data types defined by the creator of that part of the tree. The tree as used in SNMP is defined in text files that are human-readable, provided the human has the skill to puzzle them out.

---

5   ASN.1 was successful enough that the International Telecommunications Union felt no need to create ASN.2. Everyone capitulated in terror of what the ITU might do next.

Each entry is represented by a period and a number. SMI resembles a directory tree: `.9.8.7` could be thought of as */9/8/7*. Most of these numbers also have names, for easier human comprehension. We'll see how to translate between words and numbers in Chapter 3. Each entry has more definition information, such as data types, that we'll learn about later.

SNMP mostly uses the part of the ASN.1 tree beginning with the OID `.1.3.6.1`, or `.iso.org.dod.internet`. The first `.1`, or `.iso`, represents the part of the ASN.1 tree managed by the International Standards Organization, or ISO. The 3, or `org`, represents organizations within ISO. 6, or `dod`, is for the US Department of Defense. (Remember, SNMP was created when the DoD was among the Internet's primary users.) The second 1, or `internet`, represents the Internet. (Chapter 3 teaches you to translate between numbers and names as needed.) I want to say that you don't need to worry about objects outside `.1.3.6.1`, but if you're trying to use SNMP to monitor power or telecommunications systems you'll encounter those OIDs. Nations have their own chunks of these OIDs—for example, `.2.16.124` is Canada. These alien Objects from the Great Beyond have the same structure and rigidly defined data types as the more familiar OIDs, however.

Most modern SNMP takes place under `.1.3.6.1.2.1`, a part of the MIB tree known as `mib-2`. Many SNMP commands and programs assume that everything happens under `mib-2`, and default to not showing those parts of the OID. Dropping those twelve characters might seem unnecessary, but if you're groveling around in the detritus under `.iso.org.dod.internet.mgmt.mib-2.ip.ip-Forward.ipCidrRouteTable.ipCidrRouteEntry.ip-CidrRouteDest` you want to save all the screen space you can.

One common complaint about OIDs is that they're so long and complex. It's a perfectly valid lament, but; the real world is complex.

Any hierarchical scheme for displaying system internals would wind up looking a lot like ASN.1 and SMI. Many (not all) of SNMP's problems have nothing to do with these organizational systems, but with the ramshackle MIB definitions and lackadaisical agent implementations begrudgingly offered by indifferent vendors.

You can shorten many object names by using a unique name within a module. You'll see objects with names like `HOST-RE-SOURCES-MIB::hrMemorySize.0`. The module `HOST-RE-SOURCES-MIB` contains a whole bunch of objects defined in a specific standard. They're probably in a text document called `HOST-RESOURCES-MIB.txt` somewhere on your host. This full name of `HOST-RESOURCES-MIB::hrMemorySize.0` is `.iso.org.dod.internet.mgmt.mib-2.host.hrSystem.hrMemorySize.0`, or `.1.3.6.1.2.1.25.2.2.0`. While you could cope with the long name, and you could look up the numbers, using a module name like `HOST-RESOURCES-MIB` is a little easier to read and might—*might*—offer a hint what this object is for.

Most MIBs contain categories of items. If you see an OID like `.1.3.6.1.2.1.25.2.3.1.1`, it's a good bet that there's a next OID like `.1.3.6.1.2.1.25.2.3.1.2`. Some OIDs are truly standalone, though; the next OID is in a different part of the MIB tree. Standalone OIDs typically end in `.0`, and are usually scalar values.

Individual objects from different MIBs can be interleaved among each other, as we'll see later this chapter. Objects are defined in a specific order, and SNMP should always report them in that order, but the MIB defining what those objects represent is more flexible.

Object Data Types

While the MIB defines the standard for objects, the agent provides those objects to managers. Your SNMP manager can say "Hey, agent, what's the value of the OID `.1.3.6.1.2.1.25.1`?" The agent, in turn, spits out an answer. The answer must use the data type defined by the MIB, using one of the data types permitted by SMI-2 and the SNMP protocol version. Your agent reads the MIB and interprets the response in accordance with the defined data structure. For example, I queried an agent for how long it's been running and got an answer of:

```
Timeticks: (1036424800) 119 days, 22:57:28.00
```

This answer is in the unit "timeticks." My manager helpfully put the agent's answer in parentheses and translated timeticks into clock time for me.

The MIBs define a common standard for everyone to communicate with, so that agents and managers written by different entities can communicate with each other. The MIB designer is responsible for assigning data types that make sense for the object. I have seen organizations define every object in a MIB as containing an arbitrary string, forcing the manager to parse those strings to obtain useful data. This lets the team responsible for implementing the agent be sloppy, but grants anyone attempting to use said agent a lifetime pass to Gibbering Lunacy. These organizations are part of why SNMP has a bad reputation.

The definition in the MIB file must match the implementation in the agent. Many vendors fall down here. Even if the vendor has a conscientious SNMP team, other developers frequently create systems without ever considering that someone might want to monitor them. It'll be up to you to figure out exactly what the MIB exposes. Sorting out differences between the definition and the agent is perhaps the greatest annoyance of working with SNMP.

Here are some of the common units you'll see. A few other types exist, but they're either rare or obsolete.

Timeticks are one hundredth of a second. This is a 32-bit number, so its maximum value is a little over 497 days. Timeticks are almost always used for timekeeping.

An *integer* or *integer32* is a signed 32-bit number, ranging from -2,147,483,648 to 2,147,483,647. Agents use integers for all sorts of things.

A *string* contains either binary or text data, and most implementations and most MIBs restrict it to 255 characters or less. You'll see a couple variants on this: *DisplayString* is restricted to ASCII characters, while *octet string* includes binary.

An *Object Identifier* or *OID* data type is literally another OID. An object that points at another OID helps glue different parts of the MIB tree together.

IP Address represents a literal IPv4 address, used for networking. It's mostly used for routing and sockets.

Counter32 and *counter64* are 32-bit and 64-bit counters. Counters start at 0 and only increase. They're used to count something, such as the number of packets sent or the number of memory allocation failures. When a counter reaches its maximum value, it loops back to zero. You'll often see these used for errors, packets, and so on. SNMPv1 is based on SMI-1, and doesn't include counter64. Counter64 is sometimes abused into serving as the non-existent 64-bit integer.

The data type *Gauge32* can increase and decrease. Agents use gauges for current levels of something, such as the current network utilization or the instantaneous swap space usage. The MIB can define maximum and minimum values for these, and an agent might impose its own limits. Sadly, there is no 64-bit gauge counter.

Remember the difference between counters and gauges by thinking of automobiles. Odometers are counters. Speedometers are gauges.

Walking the MIB

You're not going to read MIB files to see what information a host can export through SNMP. Don't get me wrong, you *could*—but you're not going to. There's no way to see if a device truly supports the entire MIB without querying the device. Realistically, you're going to use a manager program like snmpbulkwalk(1) or SnmpB to query a device and see what it spews out. Your manager will read the MIB files and interpret each object it receives as per the definition in the file.

Chapter 3 covers performing queries, but "walking" the MIB tree generates output much like this.

```
SNMPv2-MIB::sysDescr.0 = STRING: RouterOS RB2011iL
SNMPv2-MIB::sysObjectID.0 = OID: SNMPv2-SMI::enterprises.14988.1
DISMAN-EVENT-MIB::sysUpTimeInstance =
        Timeticks: (1036424800) 119 days, 22:57:28.00
SNMPv2-MIB::sysContact.0 = STRING: nobody@mwl.io
SNMPv2-MIB::sysName.0 = STRING: 2019mainrouter
SNMPv2-MIB::sysLocation.0 = STRING: primary datacenter
...
```

You could split the several thousand lines of output into two columns, separated by the equals sign. The left side gives the OID, while the right side is the value. Our first OID is `SNMPv2-MIB::sysDescr.0`, or `.1.3.6.1.2.1.1.1.0`. This is the `sysDescr` entry within the `SNMPv2-MIB` part of the tree. The MIB definition declares that all valid entries are of type *string*. This object has a value of *RouterOS RB2011iL*. I happen to know that the router separating my test lab from my production and IoT networks is a variant of the Mikrotik RouterBoard RB2011. The "sysDescr" stands for "system description," and the value is the model of the device the agent runs on. Mind you, certain vendors use descriptions containing only the company name.

The second line is the OID `SNMPv2-MIB::sysObjectID.0`, or `.1.3.6.1.2.1.1.2.0`. The valid values are of type OID. This is an object that points at another object. The value of this object is `SNMPv2-SMI::enterprises.14988.1`, or `.1.3.6.1.4.1.14988.1`. This object is for vendor-specific MIBs; it's telling the manager "If you want to know the vendor-specific information, poke here."

The third line is `DISMAN-EVENT-MIB::sysUpTimeInstance`, also known as `.1.3.6.1.2.1.1.3.0`, and comes from a wholly separate MIB standard. An Internet search for `DISMAN-EVENT-MIB` takes you to the definition file *DISMAN-EVENT-MIB.txt*, which in turn points at RFC 2981. Digging around in that arcane doc-

ument informs us that this MIB represents the system uptime. Its legitimate values are all *Timeticks*, which are hundredths of a second. This
router has been running for *1036424800* hundredths of a second, or
119 days and change. This object also appears in SNMPv2-MIB, but
my MIB files parsed so that the definition on DISMAN-EVENT-MIB
appears, as discussed in Chapter 4.

In addition to understanding how SNMP can drive sysadmins to
madness, we can already see why SNMP interests intruders. These first
two entries reveal the router's model and uptime. Have any security
problems been found in the Routerboard RB2011iL in the last 119
days? If so, any disreputable visitor has hints of where to start poking.

The fourth entry, SNMPv2-MIB::sysContact.0 or
.1.3.6.1.2.1.1.4.0, offers a string and has a value of
nobody@mwl.io. This is the system contact information, or who to
contact when this host starts spewing garbage across your network.

We have two different parts of the MIB tree intermingled here:
SNMPv2-MIB, DISMAN-EVENT-MIB, and back to SNMPv2-MIB.
But look at the numerical values.

```
.1.3.6.1.2.1.1.1.0
.1.3.6.1.2.1.1.2.0
.1.3.6.1.2.1.1.3.0
.1.3.6.1.2.1.1.4.0
```

These MIBs are in numerical order. You can make the ordering
clearer by walking the SNMP tree and viewing all the MIBs by number
rather than by name, but that takes data that's already fairly occult and
obscures it from all but the most enlightened.

Note that these OIDs all end in .0. They are terminal branches.
When an OID ends in .0, there's no point in looking for a sibling .1 af-
terwards. It doesn't exist.

These few lines present data of interest, though. Your network
management system can interrogate the system uptime MIB every few
minutes. If that number ever goes back to zero, your host either re-

booted or its time counter rolled over. Graphing this MIB makes many service interruptions incredibly obvious.

Other data is not so obvious.

Object Groups

A MIB might batch a bunch of related object together as a *group*. Each group has its own object, but it's purely organizational. You will never see that object in a walk. The group has no value. You can query by the group name or OID, though.

The best known group is the `system` group. We saw the start of the `system` group in the previous section. It contains basic information about the host: what's its hostname? What operating system does it run? Whom do I contact for problems with the host? What SNMP MIBs does it support? That last might not be important for non-SNMP applications, but the SNMP manager needs to know what it can expect the agent to provide.

Tables

Some groups are very specifically formatted. Here's a weird-looking group, `if`.

```
IF-MIB::ifName.1 = STRING: ether1-home
IF-MIB::ifName.2 = STRING: ether2-lab
...
IF-MIB::ifName.10 = STRING: ether10
IF-MIB::ifName.11 = STRING: bridge
IF-MIB::ifInMulticastPkts.1 = Counter32: 0
IF-MIB::ifInMulticastPkts.2 = Counter32: 0
...
IF-MIB::ifInMulticastPkts.10 = Counter32: 0
IF-MIB::ifInMulticastPkts.11 = Counter32: 0
IF-MIB::ifInBroadcastPkts.1 = Counter32: 0
IF-MIB::ifInBroadcastPkts.2 = Counter32: 0
...
IF-MIB::ifInBroadcastPkts.10 = Counter32: 0
IF-MIB::ifInBroadcastPkts.11 = Counter32: 0
...
```

This is a whole bunch of different objects, each with add-on indexes running from 1 to 11.

Following that we have hundreds of lines of horrific crud that all follow a similar format. There's an object OID, followed by a number from 1 to 11. You'll see objects like `IF-MIB::ifName`, `IF-MIB::ifInMulticastPkts`, `IF-MIB::ifAlias`, and `IF-MIB::ifHighSpeed`, each followed with a number from 1 to 11. There are one hundred and sixty-five lines of this stuff.

This group is an *SNMP table*, `ifXTable`. It represents the system interfaces. (There's also an older interface table, `ifTable`, that isn't useless but isn't broadly suitable for monitoring modern systems.) Each name like `ifName`, `ifInMulticastPkts`, and so on, is a column in the table.

The index numbers one through eleven define which row this particular object goes on. This particular table assigns an index to each interface on the host. The first interface is named `ether1-home`, and is assigned index 1. Looking at row 1 gives you this interface's information for every column.

This one hundred sixty five separate objects is really a table with eleven rows and fifteen columns. It's an SNMP spreadsheet. When you see a list of objects like this, immediately think "table" and break open a MIB browser that displays tables. We'll see how net-snmp does that in Chapter 3. Or, you can tediously trawl through the objects for each device and hand-assemble your own interpretation of the data, as I did for a decade before I realized table-building tools existed. Whatever works for you.

Once you know tables exist, you'll want to know which tables your agent provides. You can either search the relevant MIB files for table entries, walk the SNMP tree and look for suspicious entries, or check the vendor documentation.[6]

---

6   The statement "check the vendor documentation" should always be spoken with derision.

When multiple tables share elements in common, the indexes are almost always consistent between the tables. For example, agents provide both a modern interface table (`ifXTable`) and a table of IP addresses on the host (`ipAddrTable`). The IP address table identifies underlying interfaces by their index number in the interface table. The MIB should enforce this, as it simplifies adding new columns to an already published table. We'll use this in Chapter 7 to investigate and disable unconfigured interfaces.

Network Transport

SNMP agents use UDP port 161 by default. You can assign alternate ports easily enough, but if someone has compromised your network enough to sniff packets, they will have zero trouble identifying your new SNMP port.

Using UDP gives SNMP interesting capabilities. Remember, UDP is not a worse protocol than TCP; it's for protocols that don't fit TCP's flexible but generic timeouts and handshakes. A simple SNMP operation completes within a single packet each way, where TCP needs several. This means that an SNMP request can penetrate a congested network more easily than any TCP protocol. If your web server has gone amok and is monopolizing your host, logging in over SSH might be impossibly slow, plagued by disconnects, and generally unusable. If you can manage the host via SNMP, you can shut it down in one or two stateless packets.

You can choose to run SNMP over TCP. It's almost always slower than UDP, however. If you use it for monitoring, it will also multiply the amount of traffic traversing your network. Network management traffic is most vital when the network is unstable. Don't only consider how SNMP traffic over TCP will impact your network during routine operation; think about what will happen if your network develops issues. UDP-based SNMP can still function on a network with 20% packet loss, while TCP is fickle at best in such conditions.

SNMP also supports transports like TLS, TLS over UDP (DTLS), and SSH. People have (understandably) hoped that these standards would replace raw SNMP queries over the network. The standards have been out for over a decade, though, and adoption is tiny. Common perception is that wrapping SNMP inside TLS combines the disadvantages of SNMP with the disadvantages of running a certificate authority, and major equipment vendors have chosen to avoid them. Some vendors still release equipment that supports only SNMPv1. User-based SNMPv3 security is here for the foreseeable future. Some SNMPv3 devices only support weak encryption algorithms, mind you.

Protocol Components

The SNMP protocol is built around a tiny handful of operations. The manager (the software used to configure and monitor other hosts) issues GET, GETBULK, GETNEXT, and SET. Agents can send TRAP and INFORM. You'll also see RESPONSE.

Managers use a GET to ask an agent for the value of a specific object. If your monitoring system asks your router how much traffic has passed through a single interface, it uses a GET.

Before a manager can use a GET, it needs to know which objects it can ask for. Managers and agents are often designed by different organizations and there's no way to communicate such a list beforehand. Additionally, some tables are highly dynamic and have no permanently fixed entries. The GETNEXT operation lets a manager say "Here's an OID. Tell me the OID next in line after it and the value of the object." The queried OID does not need to exist. If you GETNEXT an existing OID, it still gives you the following object rather than the one you sent. A manager can "walk" the MIB by presenting a low-numbered object and asking for the first one after it, then repeating that request for each response.

The GETBULK request lets a manager simultaneously request a bunch of GETNEXTs. Effectively it says "Run GETNEXT several times in a row and send me all the results in a single lump." GETBULK vastly accelerates mass SNMP queries. While it was introduced in SNMPv2c, some shoddy agents don't support it well. If you're doing a walk, use GETBULK whenever possible.

While all of the earlier requests read an object, some objects support being written as well as read. If a manager has read-write access and wants to tell the agent to change a value, it can issue a SET request. The agent receiving the request changes the value of the object as requested, which will probably change something on the underlying host.

Agents answer all of these with a RESPONSE.

If an agent wishes to contact a manager, it can use a TRAP message. These are most often used for log messages and alerts, but it's entirely possible to use them to trigger automated recovery.

An INFORM message is similar to a trap, but includes an acknowledgement of receipt.

Each operation traverses the network in a *Protocol Data Unit*, or *PDU*. When you're using SNMP over standard UDP, each PDU is crammed into a single packet whenever possible.

These operations are where the "simple" in SNMP's name comes from. Compared to the dozens or hundreds of moving parts in protocols like HTTP, SNMP contains very little. It's what we *do* with these parts that's not so simple.

Engine ID and Context

Every SNMPv3 agent has an engine ID. The purpose of the engine ID is to uniquely identify an SNMP agent within an organization, both on the network and on a specific host. A manager will probe the engine ID with each request, along with the time and the number of agent starts. The engine ID lets an SNMP program reject requests that erroneously reach it.

Agents can base their engine ID on characteristics like the first boot time, IP address, the MAC address of the first network interface, the phase they expect the moon to be in when lost R'lyeh rises, and whatever other data the developer could scrounge up from the system. Change any of these, and the engine ID can change. If your manage has cached the engine ID, you might need to flush that. If you're using SNMPv3 traps (Chapter 12), you must re-create the trap user.

If you explore SNMP implementations and problems, you'll eventually encounter advice to "change your engine ID and try again." This advice is meant for devices with less robust engine ID generation than net-snmp uses. You should never need to change net-snmp's engine ID. Net-snmp generates engine IDs based on the system time when it first starts and a random number. It is independent of host IP addresses, interfaces, MAC addresses, or any other long-lived-but-possibly-transitory information. If your big organization has defined a global standard for setting engine IDs in order to cope with less capable agents, obey the standard—but do so as the very first step in configuring your agent.

Similar to engine ID, an SNMPv3 agent can also have a *context*. A context is a way to differentiate information provided by different agents. An agent might be connected to multiple other agents, either as a proxy or via AgentX (Chapter 8). A manager querying the agent includes a non-default context, aiming the query at a special target. We'll use contexts briefly in Chapter 12.

Context and engine IDs are advanced use cases, which we won't broadly discuss. They're mentioned in assorted documentation, so you should be generally aware of them.

Net-SNMP Configuration

Net-snmp is the standard Unix SNMP implementation. Its license allows people to use it in other products, even with private changes, so it's also the most common embedded SNMP agent. Understanding net-snmp gives you a head start on understanding a little of what those mysterious black boxes the vendor sold to your CTO are really doing.

Many open source projects produce either a client or a server. Net-snmp is unusual in that it supplies both the agent (server) and an assortment of managers (clients). Both parts of the suite share more code than you might expect, giving each features you might expect to find only in the other part. You'd expect the agent to have logging options, but those same logging options work on the managers. Configuration file options can be used as command line options by putting a double dash (--) in front of them. (Not all command line options can be used in the configuration file.) Not only do they share a configuration syntax, you can use manager syntax in the agent configuration and vice versa. It's bewilderingly flexible.

Start by finding your configuration files.

Configuration Files and Directories

While almost every Unix vendor ships net-snmp, they've all fiddled with net-snmp's default settings. Sorting out where your Unix stuck the various net-snmp files can drive you loopy. Net-snmp includes net-snmp-config(1) to help you figure out exactly what atrocities your Unix's developers have perpetrated on the innocent[7] software. We'll refer to net-snmp-config throughout this book to help you identify default settings.

Additionally, the net-snmp toolkit is extremely customizable. It might be too customizable. The configuration files reflect this. All net-snmp commands, manager and agent alike, check several different directories for configuration files. The number and location of these directories varies by Unix version. Use the `--snmpconfpath` argument to `net-snmp-config` to identify these directories on your Unix.

```
$ net-snmp-config --snmpconfpath
/etc/snmp:/usr/share/snmp:/usr/lib64/snmp:
    /home/mwl/.snmp:/var/lib/net-snmp
```

---

7   No software is innocent. But no single piece of software has committed all crimes—except for Emacs, of course.

I'll use these directories for my examples. Not all of the directories shown are suitable for global configuration files, however.

Only files that you personally use for debugging, testing, and analysis should go under $HOME/.snmp/. The human-friendly settings you want when debugging problems probably aren't suitable for your network management system.

Net-snmp uses one file to configure managers (snmp.conf), one to configure the snmpd(8) agent (snmpd.conf), and one to configure the trap receiver (snmptrapd.conf). Additionally, it supports a .local.conf version of each: snmp.local.conf, snmpd.local.conf, and snmptrapd.local.conf. Settings in the .local.conf files override the standard .conf files.

Why do this? The first directory, usually /etc/snmp or /usr/local/etc/snmp, is for system-wide defaults. If you have settings that apply to the entire host, use the configuration file here. You can use the standard .conf file for organization-wide settings, and add additional settings specific to this server in the .local.conf file.

Many net-snmp utilities store their configuration files in share directories like /usr/share/snmp or /usr/local/share/snmp. I would not advise adding more files here, but you should be aware that tools like net-snmp-create-v3-user(1) make entries in these files.

Library directories like /usr/lib64/snmp don't normally exist, but you could create them and stash your own library-style configuration files here if you desired.

Finally, $HOME/.snmp is for each user's personal configuration files.

Net-snmp also has a persistent information directory. It contains information like SNMP user accounts, interface indexes, and all sorts of metadata that must remain consistent every time you run the program. It's almost always somewhere under /var, and generally appears last in the list. We'll discuss persistent data in Chapter 10, but for now accept that you should never edit files in this di-

rectory. Verify which directory is for persistent information with
`net-snmp-config --persistent-directory`. Back up everything in this directory, just as you would other critical system files.

Suppose you need the configuration files for the manager programs, `snmp.conf`. The possible locations on this
Unix are `/etc/snmp/snmp.conf`, `/etc/snmp/snmp.local.conf`,
`/usr/share/snmp/snmp.conf`, `/usr/share/snmp/snmp.local.conf`,
`/usr/lib64/snmp/snmp.conf`, `/usr/lib64/snmp/snmp.local.conf`,
`$HOME/.snmp/snmp.conf`, and `$HOME/.snmp/snmp.local.conf`. Settings
in each file override those in previous files.

Simplify your life by using as few of these files and directories as
possible. I recommend sticking production files in `/etc/snmp`. Use
`$HOME/.snmp` when testing on your personal system. If a library directory like `/usr/lib64/snmp` doesn't exist, do *not* create it.

Having different configuration files for different functions, some
for global settings and others for overrides, plus still more for automated setup and others for manual meddling, can be useful. Do
not get fancy while you're learning. Pick a single configuration
file and stick with it. I recommend using `/etc/snmp/snmpd.conf`
for the agent[8], `$HOME/.snmp/snmp.conf` for the manager, and
`/etc/snmp/snmptrapd.conf` for the trap collector.

Configuration Values

Each configuration file contains keywords set to values, much like
these.

```
defVersion 3
defSecurityName secureRW
defAuthPassphrase beVeryCareful
quickPrinting yes
…
```

---

8   An ancient tome from my "special" collection claims that if you put the
agent configuration in `/root/.snmp/snmpd.conf`, the Old Ones will claim you
as their plaything. Several technical reviewers attempted to verify this, but I never
heard from them again.

We'll discuss the options in each relevant section.

If an option can be either enabled or disabled, setting it to *yes, true,* or *1* turns it on. Setting it to *no, false,* or *0* turns it off. When reading the configuration, don't confuse the 1 of "true" with the numerical one.

All The Options

If you want to know what command-line or configuration options a specific version of package of a program contains, there's a couple ways to get that.

To view all the configuration file options for a program, use the -H flag. It creates a bewildering list, especially if you've never configured snmpd before. Many of those options are only intended for very special cases, though.

```
# snmpd -H
Configuration directives understood:
  In snmpd.conf and snmpd.local.conf:
    authtrapenable            1 | 2   (1 = enable, 2 = disable)
    trapsink                  host [community] [port]
    trap2sink                 host [community] [port]
    informsink                host [community] [port]
...
```

If you have a weird problem, look at the list of options and see if anything might be helpful.

To see what command-line arguments any program supports, run the command with an incorrect flag. I usually use -Q to trigger this help message.

Including Configuration Files

If the existing options for configuration files are insufficient, net-snmp configuration files can include other files by reference using the *includeFile* and *includeDir* options.

Your organization might have a standard where all SNMP agents must use a certain global configuration, maintained by an orchestration tool such as Ansible or Puppet. To include that file, use an *includeFile* directive and the file path.

```
includeFile /etc/company/company.snmpd
```

The includeFile target can use a relative path. The path is calculated from the file that includes the includeFile statement. If you want to include */etc/snmp/company.snmpd* from */etc/snmp/snmpd.conf*, you can use a path like this.

```
includeFile company.snmpd
```

Net-snmp can also read in all of the configuration files in a directory, so long as they end in *.conf*, with the *includeDir* option.

```
includeDir /etc/company/snmp/
```

Any files in */etc/company/snmp/* that end in *.conf* will get sucked into the configuration.

Using Wrong Options

Net-snmp shares a lot of code between the agent and the managers. This makes it possible to use options meant for a manager in the agent configuration file and vice versa. Do this with bracketed flags like [snmp] and [snmpd]. If you need a feature that doesn't seem to exist in the agent, but it's present in a manager, see if you can pull it over.

This option is not hard to understand once you see it, but you don't yet know enough to learn how it works. For now, merely accept that this exists. We'll do this in Chapter 10 when we configure snmpd as an AgentX subagent of itself.

Persistent Configuration

Certain net-snmp programs must maintain state between runs—notably, the agent snmpd(8). When you set up SNMPv3 users, the agent must stash those user accounts somewhere. Also, host-level changes can alter the information the agent provides. The agent must track state so that such information remains consistent after such changes. For example, SNMP's network interface MIB assigns an index number to each network interface. You want that index number to remain consistent across reboots.

Net-snmp tracks such information in a *persistent* data file, named the same as the program's primary configuration file. The agent's persistent configuration file is named `snmpd.conf`. See where your Unix puts this file by running `net-snmp-config` with the `--persistent-directory` flag.

```
$ net-snmp-config --persistent-directory
/var/net-snmp
```

You might notice that this directory appears on the list of directories net-snmp searches for configuration files.

While you can read the persistent data file, you should never edit it. It is intended for net-snmp programs to store their private information. While the persistent data files look like any other net-snmp configuration file, they start with a great big reminder that you shouldn't edit them. Take that advice.

You can change the location of the persistent data directory, using environment variables like $SNMP_PERSISTENT_FILE, $SNMP-CONFPATH, or $SNMP_PERSISTENT_DIR, and the *persistentDir* configuration setting. We'll do this in Chapter 10 when we use AgentX to work around performance problems, but for most of us it's unwise.

Net-snmp daemons read the persistent data file at startup and write it at shutdown, or when they get a SIGHUP. If you make a change that alters persistent data, you must signal the daemon.

Aggregating Configuration Files

So any net-snmp program potentially reads a dozen configuration files, in one of several directories that vary by operating system. Later directories override earlier directories, and `.local` files override other files. How are you supposed to tell what the program is actually doing, other than running it and seeing what incomprehensible things happen? Use snmpconf(1).

The snmpconf(1) program is most commonly used to configure agents and trap receivers. It has the ability to read existing configuration files, though, and spit out a file containing all the options that get used. It also comments those options. It creates files named `snmp.conf`, `snmpd.conf`, and/or `snmptrapd.conf`, which means you must either take care to not run this program in a configuration directory or tell it to put the newly created files elsewhere. If you run this while you're in `/etc/snmp`, and don't specify a different directory to put the files in, `snmpconf` will overwrite your existing files. You probably don't want that.

Use -a to tell snmpconf to skip the configuration questions. The -r flag lets you specify which existing files it should examine. Adding -r all tells it to suck in everything it knows about. Finally, use -I and a directory to have it write files to that directory. Here, I have the new file written in the directory `/tmp/snmp`.

```
$ snmpconf -a -r all -I /tmp/snmp
I can create the following types of configuration files
for you. Select the file type you wish to create:
(you can create more than one as you run this program)

  1:   snmpd.conf
  2:   snmptrapd.conf
  3:   snmp.conf

Other options: quit

Select File:
```

We'll be working with the manager before the agent, so I choose 3 to set up `snmp.conf`.

```
The configuration information which can be put into
snmp.conf is divided into sections.  Select a configura-
tion section for snmp.conf that you wish to create:
  1:   Debugging output options
  2:   Textual mib parsing
  3:   Output style options
  4:   Default Authentication Options

Other options: finished
Select section: finished
```

We don't want to create any new configuration. The snmpconf program has pulled in the existing files, and we just want the ones that apply written to a file. Enter "finished."

```
I can create the following types of configuration files
for you. Select the file type you wish to create:
(you can create more than one as you run this program)

   1:   snmp.conf
   2:   snmpd.conf
   3:   snmptrapd.conf

Other options: quit
```

You could aggregate the other files if you wish, but for our purposes we can enter "quit."

```
The following files were created:

   snmp.conf installed in /tmp/snmp
```

The aggregated file contains descriptions of every option, letting you easily review your effective settings. This feature makes net-snmp's multi-directory flexibility manageable, or lets you easily migrate away from that to a single monolithic configuration.

Net-SNMP Command-Line Arguments

The net-snmp manager commands have a whole bunch of common features, and most command-line arguments work across all manager programs. The most universal are documented in snmpcmd(1).

Some arguments group features by function, and have additional arguments of their own. The output modifier -O is one example. On its own, -O does nothing. It is followed by additional flags, though, that trigger particular output modifications. You'll see instructions like "use -Oa to enable this, or -Ob to show output this way." There's also an input modifier, -I, that takes flags to change how commands treat arguments.

The −c flag is reserved for program-specific commands. While −Ci tells snmptable(1) to include the index number in a table, that same flag tells snmpbulkwalk(1) to include the requested object in the output. Remember that −C is program-dependent. You can stack arguments to −C as needed, as in −Cbiw. You can use multiple −C arguments when those arguments need even more parameters.

Net-SNMP Modules

Net-snmp releases new versions every few years. It's fairly stable software. The agent has many optional components, or *modules*, that can be disabled at compilation time. It's not uncommon to discover that a feature won't work on your Unix because the packager decided to disable a module the net-snmp developers normally make a default.

The net-snmp-config command includes an option to list everything built into your particular agent binary, --snmpd-module-list. A regular net-snmp install includes almost 200 modules, and they all get spilled out in a single hard-to-read line, separated by spaces. Break that up into single lines with xargs(1), and save the list for future reference.

```
$ net-snmp-config --snmpd-module-list |\
    xargs -n 1 > snmpd.modules.list
```

The module list contains entries like this.

```
mibII/mta_sendmail
mibII/tcpTable
ucd-snmp/diskio
host/hrh_storage
...
```

At this moment, my net-snmp has 182 modules. Each entry starts with the category, then the actual module name. The modules we see here are *mta_sendmail*, *tcpTable*, *diskio*, and *hrh_storage*. Unfortunately, there's no central list of what the various modules mean. You must use your familiarity with SNMP, MIBs, and systems administration to figure them out. Modules are often named after the feature that they support, such as *diskio* in this list. Advanced users can disable modules at snmpd startup with the `-I` flag, which we'll see an example of in Chapter 10.

If an snmpd feature doesn't work, verify your Unix packager included the relevant module. If it's missing, try to discover why. Perhaps that module doesn't work well on your Unix, or maybe it merely annoyed a developer at the wrong moment.

We'll also use modules for setting up snmpd as a subagent (Chapter 10).

Now let's set up manager access to an agent.

Chapter 2: Authentication

A common complaint is that SNMP has poor authentication and transport security. That's true, if you use standards that were obsoleted early this millennium. To use SNMPv3's strong authentication and privacy you must create SNMPv3 users, configure the agent, and add those users to the manager. Once you understand SNMPv3, we'll discuss older versions for those despairing folks trapped in ancient aeons.

SNMPv3 Users

Most sysadmins trying SNMPv3 go wrong by leaping straight to configuring their agent to use the protocol and deferring the issue of user management. This is precisely backwards. You cannot configure the agent if you don't understand users.

SNMPv3 has several security paradigms, but the only widely deployed one is the *User Security Module*, or *USM*. A user isn't merely a username and password. It is a description of how that user exchanges authentication and queries between manager and agent. This isn't entirely unique; many operating systems include password hashing algorithms in password files.

Creating users is a separate process from granting them access. You'll create users with tools like snmpusm(1) and net-snmp-create-v3-user(1). You'll grant those users access with entries in `snmpd.conf`.

The user database resides on the SNMP agent. The manager must have a bunch of information about the user to access the agent, but the nitty-gritty details are all stored on the agent. The most annoying of these details probably involve encryption.

Encryption and Interoperability

A big requirement of SNMP is interoperability. Your manager must be able to interact with all sorts of devices. This drove a bunch of decisions on how SNMP uses encryption.

In your typical authentication system, a single entity controls the entire system. Your Unix manages `/etc/passwd`. A web site's database backend stores password hashes. Software attempting to access these resources either knows what algorithm they use, or relies on server features to get the correct information. Any deviance is an error punishable by rejection. On the rare occasions you must copy your password file from one Unix to another, or change database engines, you must carefully examine the encrypted and hashed data so that the new software can accept it. It's a substantial project.

With SNMP, different entities control different agents. Maybe ShoggothCorp routers support the current standard set of algorithms, while Nightgaunt switches support the up-and-coming hotness. The new CentOS uses modern algorithms, but you have a decades-old Sun Solaris server subject to federal regulations and you literally cannot upgrade it without Congressional legislation.

Additionally, everything changes over time. Folks are adding AES256 and 3DES encryption into SNMP, although some implementations are not interoperable. The current algorithms are fine today, but won't be in another decade. It'll take longer than that to cycle most of the current gear out of use.

An agent needs to record what managers can use which encryption methods and security levels. The protocol designers chose to incorporate this information into user accounts.[9]

User Security Levels and Algorithms

SNMP defines three levels of communications security: unauthenticated (also called *noAuthNoPriv* or *noauth*), authenticated (*authNoPriv* or *auth*), and private (*authPriv* or *priv*). These security levels are separate from permissions to access different agent functions, although more powerful access usually requires greater communications security.

---

9   Were there other ways to solve this problem? Sure. Not better ways, though. Not even less painful ways. You have to deal with this *somewhere*.

Under noAuthNoPriv, no traffic is encrypted. The user is completely unauthenticated. All traffic is exchanged in clear text. Managers might demand you enter a password, but it can be blank. NoAuthNoPriv behaves much like community names in older versions of SNMP.

With authNoPriv, SNMP adds a hash of the entire packet so the packet can't be altered without detection. The password isn't sent, but it's used to generate the key that authenticates the hash.

Finally, authPriv encrypts the exchange. The username is sent in plain text, but the contents of the query and the response are encrypted. You must use authentication to have privacy.

Additionally, authentication and privacy use separate algorithms. Today's authentication commonly hashes passwords via either MD5 or some variant on SHA. Privacy encrypts the query and response with either DES or an AES variant. For a user to function properly, both the manager and the agent must share the same username, password, and algorithms for authentication and privacy. Agent and manager must also agree on permitted authentication and privacy settings. If a manager says a user uses authNoPriv but the agent requires authPriv, or one says DES while the other says AES128, the user won't get access. Settings are not negotiated: if a manager uses incorrect settings, the agent sees only an authentication failure and rejects the request.

Both authentication and privacy use *passphrases* to secure traffic. A passphrase is a password that can include spaces as well as numbers and symbols. The examples in this book do not include spaces, because spaces must be escaped on the command line and the examples herein already sufficiently damage the reader's brain. A user can have different authentication and privacy passphrases, the same passphrase for both, or no passphrases, depending on your network's threat model. Passphrases must be at least eight characters long, but not all vendors enforce this restriction. Maximum length varies by vendor.

Production authentication and privacy passphrases should differ, especially when your equipment restricts you to weaker algorithms. You don't want an intruder who cracks your MD5 authentication passphrase to get your DES passphrase for free.

Templates and Accounts

According to the SNMP standards, user accounts are created from template accounts. You create a template to define the authentication and privacy algorithms. Template accounts can authenticate to the agent, and can be assigned permissions. Creating a routine user account means cloning that template and changing the passphrases. Theoretically, a template user shouldn't be used for normal operations.

As far as usage is concerned, there's no real difference between a template account and a regular account. Many vendors feel gleefully unconstrained by this "clone new users from templates" standard. They could technically declare that all of their accounts are templates, and that templates are usable.

Don't be surprised if an agent requires you to clone users from a template. Don't be surprised if it lets you create individual users. Don't be surprised if template accounts can't be used for normal operations, or if they can be. Surrender to your vendor's will and move on with your life.

User Creation Checklist

Before trying to create a user, verify that you have:

- a username
- a privacy level (noauth, authNoPriv, or authPriv)
- if using authNoPriv or authPriv, an authentication encryption method (MD5 or SHA) and passphrase
- if using authPriv, a privacy encryption method (DES or AES)and passphrase

Before creating the user, verify that both agent and manager can handle all of your choices. While these are all defined in the standard, you never know what horrors a vendor might invoke in the name of "security," profits, or ignorance.

Creating users requires bootstrapping a template user, testing that user, and copying that user to create end-user accounts.

Bootstrapping Embedded Agent Users

Embedded device agents either come with an initial SNMPv3 user or have an interface to create that initial user. Once you have that user, you can use tools like snmpusm(1) to manage further accounts.

Simple embedded devices, like IPMI agents, often use a web form to create SNMPv3 users. Many won't offer a choice of encryption algorithms; you take what you're given. The simplest permit only a single SNMPv3 user in their interface, although you might be able to create more with snmpusm(1) as discussed later. Some require disabling and re-enabling the SNMP service before the user account will work.

Using accounts requires all of the information listed in the "User Creation Checklist" in the previous section. If the information isn't available in the agent interface, check the vendor documentation.

Remember, default accounts are dangerous. Use any default account to create a new administrative account. Verify that account works, and use that account to disable the default account.

Bootstrapping Net-SNMP Users

Net-snmp's agent, snmpd(8), stores users internally. As with all standard SNMPv3 user databases, they're accessible via SNMP under usmUserTable. The catch is, net-snmp expects you to use SNMP to manage that table. Net-SNMP does not provide a default privileged SNMP user, or even the standard community names used by older versions of the protocol. You can't create your initial user with SNMP. (Some Linuxes ship with configuration files that provide minimal read access via **public**, but read-only access won't let you create users and you can't use SNMPv1 or SNMPv2c to create SNMPv3 users.)

Additionally, the standard SNMP-based user setup assumes that you're cloning users that use the default settings. If you must customize a user's security level or encryption methods, you must create a template user with those defaults.

This means you'll use one method to bootstrap the user database and create new template users. You'll use a wholly different method to clone new users from those templates.

Creating Initial and Template Users

If you've never created users before, use the net-snmp-create-v3-user tool to ease the process. Whenever you need a template user that has unique encryption algorithms, you must follow this as well. It requires snmpd be stopped first.

service snmpd stop

Now use net-snmp-create-v3-user(1) to create the account.

Specify the authentication algorithm with -a and the privacy algorithm with -x. Here I create a user that uses SHA-256 and AES128, with the common passphrase *securePassword*. (If you're running net-snmp 5.7 or older, use plain SHA and AES instead.) The username is **templateshaaes**, to indicate it's a template that uses SHA and AES.

**net-snmp-create-v3-user -a SHA-256 -x AES128 \
    templateshaaes**

It will prompt you for an authentication passphrase. Enter it. When it prompts you for a privacy passphrase, hitting ENTER will reuse the authentication passphrase.

If you want to specify passphrases on the command line, use -A for the authentication passphrase and -X for the privacy passphrase. If you use -A but not -X, net-snmp-create-v3-user reuses the authentication password for privacy.

The command prints out exactly what changes it makes.

```
adding the following line to /var/net-snmp/snmpd.conf:
   createUser templateshaaes SHA-256 "securePassword" AES128
adding the following line to /usr/local/share/snmp/snmpd.conf:
   rwuser templateshaaes
```

The first two lines show that the command added a *createUser* statement to `/var/net-snmp/snmpd.conf`. This creates the user in the persistent data file, which you should never edit by hand.

The last two lines show that the command added a *rwuser* statement to `/usr/local/share/snmp/snmpd.conf`, granting our new user access to the agent. Note that this is *not* the primary configuration file; you might want to move this entry to the primary file later. This entry gives our new user read-write access to the agent.

Start snmpd.

 # service snmpd start

The agent will read its instructions and create your first SNMPv3 user. If you get an error, you probably made your authentication key too short.

The bootstrap user creation method does not permit editing users, changing passphrases or encryption methods, or other standard user activities. It exists only to initialize the user database and provide an initial template user. You can use snmpusm(1) to manage users on many SNMPv3 agents.

Bootstrapping Users Manually

You can bootstrap SNMPv3 users without using net-snmp-create-v3-user(1), but it requires two file edits. Use the *createUser* `snmpd.conf` keyword to create users and the *rwuser* keyword to grant it access to the agent.

```
createUser user authalgo "authpassphrase" privalgo "privpassphrase"
rwuser user
```

The user is the SNMPv3 username. Set the authentication algorithm next, followed by the authentication passphrase in quotes. Then we have the privacy algorithm, followed by the quoted privacy passphrase.

If the *createUser* keyword is added to the persistent data file, as net-snmp-create-v3-user does, snmpd creates the user and overwrites the cleartext passphrases with the scrambled versions. You cannot edit the persistent data file, however, so you must alter the standard configuration file in `/etc/snmp/snmpd.conf`. Snmpd cannot alter that file. Your entry, unencrypted passphrases and all, stays visible to anyone who can access `snmpd.conf`.

Taken all together, manually bootstrapping users requires adding a *createUser* and *rwuser* statement to `/etc/snmp/snmpd.conf`, restarting snmpd, and removing that *createUser* statement from `snmpd.conf`. Best practice says to restart the service any time you touch its configuration file, so perform one more restart.

Your user database is now bootstrapped.

Testing Users Against Agents

Verify that the newly created initial/template users can communicate with the agent. We used a *rwuser* keyword to activate the account, but configured no other access control. You can now use your first SNMP manager command. All the manager commands net-snmp includes use the same command-line format:

```
# command <options> <agent> <command-specific-flags>
```

The options must come first. Following the options is the agent, or the host you're querying. Finally, commands have options that might appear after the agent, such as a specific OID to tweak. Here's an example of using the net-snmp template user to check the MIB on our test host, from our test host, with the snmpstatus(1) command.

```
$ snmpstatus -v 3 -l priv -u templateshaaes \
    -A securePassword -a SHA-256 -X securePassword \
    -x AES128 localhost
[UDP: [127.0.0.1]:161->[0.0.0.0]:30148]=>[FreeBSD
    freebsd 12.0-RELEASE-p10 FreeBSD 12.0-RELEASE-p10
    GENERIC amd64] Up: 1 day, 4:08:18.78
Interfaces: 2, Recv/Trans packets: 1317065/870014 |
    IP: 191548/134076
```

The snmpstatus(1) command is a "Hello? Is this thing on?" tool. If it spits out some basic information about your host, your authentication is set up correctly and your agent is running. You must manage authentication on the command line until we set up agent configuration files.

The -v flag gives the SNMP version to use. We're using an SNMPv3 user, so use -v 3.

Use -l to set the security level. Our user supports both authentication and privacy, so we use -l priv.

Give the username with -u.

The -A flag lets you enter the user's authentication password, and -a lets you give the authentication algorithm. Our password is *securePassword*, and the algorithm is SHA-256.

Use -X to give the user's privacy password, and -x to set the algorithm. The privacy password is also *securePassword*, and the algorithm is AES128.

Finally, give the agent to query. We're querying the host we're running on, so use **localhost**.

If you get an "authentication failure" or "no response" message, you entered the incorrect username, password, or encryption method.

Managing Users with snmpusm

Once you have template users, you can manage users on a running system with snmpusm(1). Additionally, snmpusm can be used remotely—your manager can edit users on all the agents it has access to. It *should* work on any agent, not just net-snmp agents.

Creating a production user requires cloning a template user and setting new passphrases for the account. This two-step shuffle, and most of the other user management dances, are mandated by the SNMP standards rather than the net-snmp developers. The net-snmp team did not design this process to torment you; those torments were strongly recommended by the protocol designers. Any other implementations either have the same requirements, obscure what they're really doing in the hope that you'll like them, or have abandoned the standards.

What happens when you must change a user's authentication and privacy encryption methods? You can't. You can delete the user, and create a new user of the same name from a different template, but you can't change the original user. Suppose you deploy a ShoggothCorp manager that uses MD5 for authentication and DES for privacy. All of your agents have a template user named **templatemd5des** to provide those settings. The account **shoggoth** is a clone of that user, with authentication and privacy passphrases added. Several years later, ShoggothCorp upgrades their manager to use SHA and AES. You can't go into your agent and change **shoggoth** to use these algorithms. You must first create a new template user, **templateshaaes**. Destroy the **shoggoth** user that uses MD5 and DES, and clone a new **shoggoth** from the SHA/AES template.

Creating Users

We'll start by creating a new user that follows the agent's defaults, whatever they are. As the standard says that usable SNMPv3 users must be cloned from template users, this user will be an template. We can use it to create users, however.

```
$ snmpusm -v3 -l priv -u templateshaaes \
   -A securePassword -X securePassword -a SHA-256 \
   -x AES128 localhost create templatedefault
```

The options on the snmpusm command looks a bunch like the snmpstatus(1) command in the last section, doesn't it? The net-snmp tools take pains to ensure that command line options are consistent across all of the commands, to the greatest extent possible. The -v, -l, and -u arguments define the SNMP version, security level, and username. The -A, -a, -X and -x options give encryption algorithms and passwords for our first user. We then have the agent, **localhost**. What's new are the snmpusm-specific options, create templatedefault. This creates a user named

templatedefault. While the user created with net-snmp-create-v3-user(1) had specific encryption and privacy settings, the user template **templatedefault** uses whatever settings the agent prefers. Remember, this won't appear in the persistent data file until you reload or restart snmpd.

Now clone one of these users for a real user. You'll need all of the user authentication that was used to create the template user. Use the create option, then give the username to create and the username to clone. I want to create a user **secureRW**, cloned from **templateshaaes**. This requires authenticating as a user. I use **templateshaaes**—remember, templates are users too!

```
$ snmpusm -v3 -l priv -u templateshaaes \
    -A securePassword -X securePassword -a SHA-256 \
    -x AES128 localhost create secureRW templateshaaes
User successfully created.
```

I will also create a user **secureRO**, for use in later examples.

This user is a perfect copy of the template user, including the passphrases. Before deploying the user, change the passphrases.

Changing User Passphrases

Much as with passwd(1), you must have the user's current passphrases to change them. This allows snmpusm to serve as a user-facing interface. You must change authentication and privacy passphrases separately.

The -Ca passwd snmpusm-specific option changes the authentication passphrase. You'll need the passwd command, the old passphrase, the new passphrase, and the username. Here user **secureRW** changes their authentication passphrase from *securePassword* to *beVeryCareful*.

```
$ snmpusm -v3 -l priv -u secureRW -A securePassword \
    -a SHA-256 -X securePassword -x AES128 -Ca \
    localhost passwd securePassword beVeryCareful secureRW
SNMPv3 Key(s) successfully changed.
```

To change the privacy password, you must use -Cx and also specify the privacy algorithm with -x. The account **secureRW** is cloned from **templateshaaes**, which uses AES128 encryption. I change the privacy password from *securePassword* to *moreCarefulThanThat*. Note that I must use the authentication passphrase.

```
$ snmpusm  -v3 -l priv -u secureRW -A beVeryCareful \
   -a SHA-256 -X securePassword -x AES-128 -Cx \
   localhost passwd securePassword moreCarefulThanThat \
   secureRW
SNMPv3 Key(s) successfully changed.
```

Repeat the process with the **secureRO** account, using different passphrases.

Before you do anything else, before you even change away from the terminal, verify that the accounts work with the new passphrases. If they work, the accounts are ready to use.

Deleting Accounts

If you stop using an account, remove it. If a user has forgotten their passphrase, delete and recreate the account. Here, I screwed up and accidentally created a **ssecureRW** user, with an extra *s* at the beginning of the name. Use snmpusm's **delete** command.

```
$ snmpusm [auth options] localhost delete ssecureRW
User successfully deleted.
```

As with any collection of users, be sure you delete unneeded usernames.

Making snmpusm Changes Permanent

When you change the user database, the changes are stored in memory. Changes are not written to permanent storage until you cleanly restart or SIGHUP snmpd.

```
# service snmpd restart
```

While you might schedule restarts, you can also use an SNMP SET to tell snmpd to update its permanent storage. We don't discuss SET

until Chapter 7 but for future reference, setting `UCD-SNMP-MIB-`
`::versionSavePersistentData.0` to 1 tells snmpd to write
its persistent data file.

Allowing net-snmp Users to Access the Agent

If you're running net-snmp's snmpd, you must also permit new accounts access in `snmpd.conf`. While this file can exist in many places,
while you're learning I recommend centralizing all configuration in
`/etc/snmp/snmpd.conf`.

For read-write access, list the user with the *rwuser* keyword. Here
I grant the user **secureRW** read-write access. While we're there, give
secureRO read-only access with the *rouser* keyword.

```
rwuser secureRW
rouser secureRO
```

Chapter 9 discusses more complex access permissions.

You must restart snmpd to make it recognize the new user.

Viewing Users

User accounts are stored in the MIB, under `usmUserTable`. We
won't get to tables until the next chapter, but for the moment grant me
your trust when I tell you this command will show them.

```
$ snmptable -Cb www1 usmUserTable
```

Using this command without all the `-a`, `-A`, `-x`, `-X`, `-u`, and `-l`
flags requires you store your authentication information in the manager, though. Let's do that next.

Storing Users in the Manager

Retyping all these different usernames, passwords, and algorithms for
different agents is a certain path to irremediable madness, or at best
carpal tunnel syndrome. Fortunately, net-snmp provides the manager
configuration file `snmp.conf` that allows you to set everything once and
forget about it.

A configuration file for any net-snmp program can appear in many locations, as discussed in Chapter 1. If you skipped that, go back and read it before proceeding. A stray configuration file you didn't know existed will ruin your whole day.

Net-snmp takes pains to ensure that all commands have consistent options and flags. Each option and flag maps to a configuration file option. Here's a complete `snmp.conf` for communicating with agents, using the account **secureRW**. These settings will become our defaults.

```
defVersion 3
defSecurityName secureRW
defAuthPassphrase beVeryCareful
defAuthType SHA-256
defPrivPassphrase moreCarefulThanThat
defPrivType AES128
defSecurityLevel authPriv
```

The *defVersion* keyword lets you set the default SNMP version. We declare that we use SNMP version 3 here. It could also be 1 or 2c.

Declare your username with *defSecurityName*.

Configure the authentication passphrase and algorithm with *defAuthPassphrase* and *defAuthType*, respectively. Set your privacy passphrase and algorithm with *defPrivPassphrase* and *defPrivType*. If both passphrases are identical, you can safely use a single *defPassphrase* entry instead.

Finally, set the security level with *defSecurityLevel*. This must be set to one of *noAuthNoPriv*, *authNoPriv*, or *authPriv*.

Per-Host Settings

Using `snmp.conf` works great when you have a single username across your entire network. Even if you're that fortunate right now, eventually standards will change and your new hardware will need different encryption algorithms. You will need per-host manager configurations.

Net-snmp uses the `hosts` subdirectory to support multiple hosts. Create such a directory in an existing configuration directory, such as $HOME/.snmp/hosts. In that directory, create a file for each agent that has a different authentication information. Name the file after the agent as it will appear on the command line, followed by .conf. My server **www.mwl.io** needs a different SNMP manager configuration.[10] It has the IP addresses 203.0.103.51 and 2001:db8::2. I don't really care about its address, because I usually type it as plain **www**.

When I run an SNMP command, I could identify my agent with any of these. As I normally type it as plain **www**, though, I'd probably put the manager information in $HOME/.snmp/hosts/www.conf. If I ever type the fully qualified host name, the error would remind me I was working too hard. While the net-snmp tools don't recognize files named after IPv6 addresses, you don't want to be typing those at the command line anyway.

To keep your eyeballs from melting, from now on all examples in this book assume you have put the authentication details in an snmp.conf file. If typing really long command lines helps you feel more in touch with the inexplicable entities that control our networks, though, feel free.

The host file does not work when the agent uses a different version of SNMP than the default. If you use v3 as your default protocol version, but a single host runs v2c, you must specify the version and community on the command line. (This is identified as bug #2611 in net-snmp and might get fixed, but it's been open for several years.)

Version 1 and 2c Communities

An "enterprise network" might be defined as a collection of equipment from the last fifty years, the oldest of which cannot be replaced without upending the whole organization. Some of that equipment probably doesn't speak SNMPv3. Some slipshod vendors feel indifferent to matters such as "reliability" and "standards compliance," and their

---

10   The reasons are too tedious to explain, but involve needing an example for this book.

SNMPv3 implementation has all the interoperability of a hurdy-gurdy and a wood chipper. In such cases, you must retreat into the obsolete land of SNMP versions 1 and 2c.

Community-based authentication works the same in both SN-MPv1 and SNMPv2c. Send a query to a device using a configured community name, and the agent will respond. No username is necessary; a community effectively combines the username and password in one easily stolen cleartext text string.

With SNMPv3, creating users and granting those users access are different things. With communities, the configuration that grants communities access creates the community. A community is simpler, and doesn't need a user's tedious security information.

Choosing Community Strings

The SNMP standards don't define requirements for community strings. They can include any characters and be of any length… except when they can't.

Almost every vendor imposes limits on community strings. Many set a maximum length. Others limit the characters you can use. Some allow you to use any characters, but certain characters must be handled specially. A few permit any characters, but using certain characters causes problems. At one time, Cisco's IOS permitted use of @ in a community string, but other Cisco devices used that character to index their interfaces. Always check your vendor manual for any restrictions on the community name.

The community string is the only authentication token required to access the host's SNMP stack. You'll almost never type this string, except when putting it in an `snmp.conf` file for your manager. Feel free to make it as complicated as your manager's limitations permit.

The community strings **public** and **private** were used back in the 1980s for read-only and read-write access respectively, and should have been banned from every network as of the 1990s. Some vendors continued enabling them by default well into the current century. Using them today will delight every script kiddie who finds you.

Enabling Communities in net-snmp

Set up a read-only community by using the *rocommunity* keyword and the community name in `snmpd.conf`. Use *rwcommunity* for read-write access. Here, the community **insecureRO** has read-only access and community **insecureRW** has read-write privileges. Add these to `/etc/snmp/snmpd.conf`.

```
rocommunity   insecureRO
rwcommunity   insecureRW
```

We'll set up more limited access control for these communities in Chapter 9.

Testing Communities

We'll test our communities with snmpget(1). As with SNMPv3 queries, the `-v` flag defines the protocol version. Use `-c` to give a community name. Then give the hostname or IP address of the agent to query, and the OID.

```
$ snmpget -v 2c -c insecureRO localhost SNMPv2-MIB::sysDescr.0
SNMPv2-MIB::sysDescr.0 = STRING: Linux
    centos.blackhelicopters.org 3.10.0-1062.1.1.el7.x86_64 #1
    SMP Fri Sep 13 22:55:44 UTC 2019 x86_64
```

This SNMP query is successful.

Storing Communities in the Manager

If you don't have SNMPv3 as your default protocol, you can put SNMP communities in host configuration files. The net-snmp tools check these files for authentication information before running a query. Here I've set up a special configuration file for the host **formless**, whose agent only speaks SNMP versions 1 and 2c, in the file `$HOME/.snmp/hosts/formless.conf`.

```
defVersion   2c
defCommunity   insecureRO
```

Whenever I point an SNMP command at the host **formless**, it will use version 2c and the community **insecureRO**. Remember, this only work if SNMPv3 isn't your default protocol.

You can now configure authentication across all versions of SNMP. Let's use this to perform some basic queries.

Chapter 3: Queries

Now that you have working authentication, we can perform SNMP queries. You can either broadly interrogate agents to see what they offer, or perform very specific queries to gather specific information.

Don't perform your very first queries against an agent on a production host, though. You have no idea how your devices will react to those queries, and some of the queries this book explores can disrupt live environments. Rather, use net-snmp's snmpd(8) on your test host. A completely unconfigured snmpd will not respond to queries, but configuring users or communities in `snmpd.conf` suffices to make snmpd answer. Verify that your test host isn't accessible to the outside world, so some script kiddie can't use it for an SNMP-based distributed denial of service attack.

All of these examples assume that you've configured authentication in `snmp.conf`. You can skip that and add in all the -v, -c, -u, -l, -a, -A, -x, and -X options and arguments and passphrases to every command if you like. It's not *my* sanity at risk. I also assume that you successfully tested your authentication with snmpstatus(1). If authentication doesn't yet work, return to Chapter 2 and set up your SNMPv3 users again.

The Art of Queries

Asking SNMP for answers is both an art and a craft. SNMP has evolved over the decades, and no tool can read your mind. Some tools have hard-coded workarounds for some of those changes, but such workarounds obscure what's really happening and always come back to bite you.

The art of SNMP queries comes down to: bludgeon the tools until you get something resembling a coherent answer. This isn't the fault of net-snmp or any other toolkit. SNMP was implemented by unnamed legions of folks at many organizations across the world. The fine work of those who knew what they were doing has been occluded by all the others, and everything interacts unpredictably.

Walking SNMP

Every vendor supports SNMP MIBs a little differently, and their documentation doesn't always offer precise details. SNMP offers a couple of methods of *walking* the MIB tree, letting you tell the agent to spill everything it knows.

An SNMP walk uses GETNEXT or GETBULK requests to methodically query an agent for all supported objects. Net-snmp includes two programs, snmpwalk(1) and snmpbulkwalk(1). A bulk walk is much faster and far more efficient than a plain walk, but is not part of SNMPv1. A bulk walk works by putting multiple GETNEXT queries inside a single SNMP request, which vastly accelerates responses. Use snmpwalk(1) for feeble agents that only support SNMPv1, and snmpbulkwalk(1) for everything else. The managers are command-line compatible except where noted.

Some devices that support SNMPv2c and SNMPv3 balk at bulk walks. You might have to fall back to snmpwalk for these devices, even though it's slower.

Running snmpbulkwalk requires only a single command-line argument, the hostname of the agent to be interrogated. Once you see how this works, you'll probably want to redirect the output to a file for easier perusal.

```
$ snmpbulkwalk proxy3
SNMPv2-MIB::sysDescr.0 = STRING: FreeBSD freebsd
        12.0-RELEASE-p10 FreeBSD 12.0-RELEASE-p10 GENERIC amd64
SNMPv2-MIB::sysObjectID.0 = OID: NET-SNMP-TC::freebsd
DISMAN-EVENT-MIB::sysUpTimeInstance =
        Timeticks: (10563166) 1 day, 5:20:31.66
SNMPv2-MIB::sysContact.0 = STRING: nobody@nowhere.invalid
SNMPv2-MIB::sysName.0 = STRING: freebsdtest
SNMPv2-MIB::sysLocation.0 = STRING: somewhere
...
```

We saw examples much like this back in Chapter 1. These are the initial objects returned every time you walk an agent. We have the OID, an equals sign, the type of information contained in the object, and object's value.

We do get some useful information. The object `SNMPv2-MIB-::sysDescr.0` tells us this host runs FreeBSD and provides the operating system release and hardware architecture. The object `SN-MPv2-MIB::sysName.0` declares this host thinks its name is **freebsdtest**.

Other than authentication information, this host has an empty *snmpd.conf* file. You might guess this from objects like `SN-MPv2-MIB::sysContact.0`, the system contact, which shows an email address of **nobody@nowhere.invalid**. Similarly, the system location given by `SNMPv2-MIB::sysLocation.0` is *somewhere*. This agent doesn't know the basic facts about its own host. We'll set these in Chapter 5.

For comparison, let's do the same query against a CentOS host. It runs net-snmp's snmpd(8), with identical configuration files and user databases.

```
$ snmpbulkwalk centostest
SNMPv2-MIB::sysDescr.0 = STRING: Linux
        centostest.blackhelicopters.org 3.10.0-1062.1.1.el7.x86_64 #1
        SMP Fri Sep 13 22:55:44 UTC 2019 x86_64
SNMPv2-MIB::sysObjectID.0 = OID: NET-SNMP-MIB::netSnmpAgentOIDs.10
DISMAN-EVENT-MIB::sysUpTimeInstance = Timeticks: (1145) 0:00:11.45
SNMPv2-MIB::sysContact.0 = STRING: root@localhost
SNMPv2-MIB::sysName.0 = STRING: centostest.blackhelicopters.org
SNMPv2-MIB::sysLocation.0 = STRING: Unknown
...
```

We would expect the system description to differ, as well as the hostname. Some of the other differences are less explicable, though. The system contact on the FreeBSD host is **nobody@nowhere.invalid**, while CentOS reports **root@localhost**. FreeBSD reports a system location of *somewhere*, while CentOS reports *Unknown*. A quick check will show that Debian reports **"Me <me@example.org>"** and *"Sitting on the Dock of the Bay"* for these objects.

None of this is insurmountable, of course; a sysadmin with any experience will instantly understand that this host is declaring "I don't know who or where I am, please help me."

These minor differences illustrate a huge point about working with SNMP, however: everybody deploys it differently. This is the same agent software, running on two different operating systems, and even there it's not consistent. Imagine the sorts of differences you'll see with different agents.

If you wrote a script to query all of the agents on your network to see if they had contact information, but it only checked for one of these two addresses, you'd miss a whole category of incompletely configured agents. Defensive scripting is always good practice. SNMP doesn't prefer defensive scripting; it *demands* it. With menaces.

Complete and Empty Walks

Occasionally I'll go on a walk and not find anything. An SNMP walk defaults to starting at the OID `.1.3.6.1.2.1`, where the basic information like host identity and operating system appear. It uses GET-NEXT and/or GETBULK requests to have the agent provide the next objects. If your manager doesn't have access to anything under that OID, you won't get anything from a walk.

To ask the agent for absolutely everything your manager has access to, start your walk at `.1`.

```
$ snmpbulkwalk www2 .1
```

This presents the entire MIB as a single integrated tree.

Different Ports

While agents normally run on UDP port 161, some devices might use a different port. This could be for organizational compliance, because a different SNMP agent is running on port 161, or because the sysadmin erroneously believes that the most loathsome entities on the Internet won't find them if they choose an off port. Specify the port number after the agent's hostname, separated by a colon.

```
$ snmpbulkwalk proxy3:1161
```

If you want to try to use TCP to connect to an agent, specify `tcp:` before the agent's hostname.

```
$ snmpbulkwalk tcp:proxy3:1161
```

All of net-snmp's manager programs support this syntax.

Interpreting Objects

Up until now, you've had to take my word for the correct interpretation of the objects behind all these OIDs. This is both unsustainable and ill-advised. Each object has a formal definition, described in a MIB file. Net-snmp ships with a collection of standard MIB files, and Chapter 4 discusses acquiring and using more. Use snmptranslate(1) to extract information from MIB files. It can perform several translations, but many are of interest only to developers.

The translation I find most useful uses the `-Td` flag. This takes an OID as an argument and provides the object's description from the MIB. Here I get the information for the object identified by SNMPv2-MIB::sysContact.0, which we saw inconsistently displayed above.

```
$ snmptranslate -Td SNMPv2-MIB::sysContact.0
SNMPv2-MIB::sysContact.0
sysContact OBJECT-TYPE
  -- FROM       SNMPv2-MIB, RFC1213-MIB
  -- TEXTUAL CONVENTION DisplayString
  SYNTAX        OCTET STRING (0..255)
  DISPLAY-HINT  "255a"
  MAX-ACCESS    read-write
  STATUS        current
  DESCRIPTION   "The textual identification of the
  contact person for this managed node, together with
  information on how to contact this person.  If no
  contact information is known, the value is the
  zero-length string."
::= { iso(1) org(3) dod(6) internet(1) mgmt(2) mib-2(1)
system(1) sysContact(4) 0 }
```

The first couple of lines spit our query back at us in various forms.

The --*FROM* line gives the MIB file (or files) that define this object. This object is defined in the original SNMPv2-MIB document as well as the MIB file defined in RFC 1213. That RFC came out in 1991; we're meddling with an Elder OID here.

The --*TEXTUAL CONVENTION* and *DISPLAY-HINT* give a hint on how to display the object in the manager.

SYNTAX describes the data type.

All of these vary greatly depending on the standard applied when the MIB was written. While there's no point in preemptively learning these, you can search for these terms if you need a hint about what the object is attempting to communicate.

The *MAX-ACCESS* field tells you how much access an agent can have to this this object. It's most commonly set to "read-only" or "read-write." A read-write statement here doesn't mean that a particular agent permits your manager to write to the object, or that the agent permits such access. It means that the MIB file snmptranslate is parsing claims that the agent allows read-write access. You might also see the value "not-accessible," meaning that this object exists to support other objects further down the tree but you can't read it via SNMP. A very few objects are "read-create," meaning that you can add objects through an SNMP SET command.

In *STATUS*, you can see if this object is considered part of the current standard, or if it's been deprecated or obsoleted. This object is current. Just because an object was deprecated in 1998 doesn't mean that your brand-new ShoggothCorp router won't offer it, however. If you're using an obsolete MIB file (Chapter 4), however, this field can mislead you.

The *DESCRIPTION* tells you what this object is for, and is what interests most of us. The description is often written in that obscure tongue "Standards-Speak" and might require a bit of deciphering. Take this one, starting with "textual identification." Text—that means words.

This object contains words. This object should contain the contact person for the host. [11] Deprecated and obsolete objects will often include hints about their replacements in the description.

The last line contains a textual and numerical interpretation of the object identifier, letting you pull it all together. This OID translates to .1.3.6.1.2.1.1.4.0. While you can piece the OID together by hand, all the SNMP commands support output modifiers with -O and a flag. Using -On tells the command to print OIDs in numerical form. Translate this OID again, but add the -On option.

```
$ snmptranslate -Td -On SNMPv2-MIB::sysContact.0
.1.3.6.1.2.1.1.4.0
sysContact OBJECT-TYPE
...
```

The first line of the output is the numerical OID.

We explore other output modifiers in "Modifying Output" later this chapter.

The Enterprise MIB

An SNMP walk starts at the OID .1.3.6.1.2.1, the first object in the SN-MPv2 MIB, and works by asking the agent over and over for the next object. Agents can have OIDs beyond this MIB. Even when SNMP seems to show you a host's underlying secrets, there's always another layer to discover. Consider the OID SNMPv2-MIB::sysObjec-tID. It returns another OID. Checking this on my FreeBSD hosts gives me:

```
SNMPv2-MIB::sysObjectID.0 = OID: NET-SNMP-TC::freebsd
```

On Centos and Debian you'll see something like this.

```
SNMPv2-MIB::sysObjectID.0 = OID: NET-SNMP-MIB::netSnmpAgentOIDs.10
```

---

11   Note the last sentence, which declares that hosts with unknown contact information should use a zero-length string here. FreeBSD, CentOS, and Debian are all equally and uniquely incorrect. In its defense, Debian inherits its incorrectness directly from net-snmp.

Poking a different device, like my lab's Mikrotik router, gives you something different still.

```
SNMPv2-MIB::sysObjectID.0 = OID: SNMPv2-SMI::enterprises.14988.1
```

Let's see what this OID means.

```
$ snmptranslate -Td SNMPv2-MIB::sysObjectID.0
```
...
```
DESCRIPTION   "The vendor's authoritative identifi-
cation of the network management subsystem contained
in the entity. This value is allocated within the
SMI enterprises subtree (1.3.6.1.4.1) and provides
an easy and unambiguous means for determining `what
kind of box' is being managed.  For example, if ven-
dor `Flintstones, Inc.' was assigned the subtree
1.3.6.1.4.1.424242, it could assign the identifier
1.3.6.1.4.1.424242.1.1 to its `Fred Router'."
```
...

This is a fancy way to say "The vendor says to look here for more information." So let's see the description of these objects.

```
$ snmptranslate -Td -On NET-SNMP-TC::freebsd
```

This translates the FreeBSD OID to .1.3.6.1.4.1.8072.3.2.8, but returns no description. Similarly, the CentOS and Debian OIDs translate to .1.3.6.1.4.1.8072.3.2.10 without a description, while Mikrotik is .1.3.6.1.4.1.14988.1.

The OID .1.3.6.1.4.1 is the top of what's known as the "enterprise MIB." Organizations can register a MIB and get their own OID under this OID. This is where they stick all their proprietary and custom stuff, often the most desirable information. When you walk an agent's MIBs, it doesn't include this tree by default.

What you find in an agent's enterprise MIB depends entirely on the agent. An embedded device manufacturer like Mikrotik, who makes a straightforward set of products, probably has a comparatively simple MIB. A massive company like Cisco, which grew ever larger by reaching into the mortal realm to engulf smaller firms entire, has dozens or hundreds of enterprise objects here—but not all devices support all of their OIDs. Net-snmp falls somewhere in the middle; they've implemented several enterprise MIBs.

Walking Specific MIBs

To view only part of the MIB tree, give the top OID after the agent. Here I want to see everything that's under .1.3.6.1.4.1, the enterprise MIB, on one of my test hosts running net-snmp's snmpd.

```
$ snmpbulkwalk proxy3 .1.3.6.1.4.1
UCD-SNMP-MIB::memIndex.0 = INTEGER: 0
UCD-SNMP-MIB::memErrorName.0 = STRING: swap
UCD-SNMP-MIB::memTotalSwap.0 = INTEGER: 2097024 kB
UCD-SNMP-MIB::memAvailSwap.0 = INTEGER: 2097024 kB
...
```

It's a whole new set of information. Stuff that the net-snmp developers thought you'd like to know about your host. Scan through this list, pick a few intriguing objects, and run snmptranslate to see what they really show. Monitoring some of these objects has saved me all sorts of trouble.

Broken Agents

Some flawed agents that should never have been unleashed upon helpless customers cannot successfully complete an SNMP walk. Somewhere in the middle of the MIB, the GETNEXT request says there's nothing else. More objects do exist, but the agent can't get to them from the break. The only way to get to the rest of the MIB is to know the OID to start at.

If your walk seems bizarrely truncated, check the documentation. If there's a support forum or mailing list, for this product see if other people have reported the failure.

SNMP Tables

SNMP presents information about entire subsystems in an organized method. The most effective way to examine such information would be a table. SNMP supports tables, but you might not recognize them as such. Tables are a key SNMP feature, and are extensively discussed in Chapter 1. Viewed with snmpbulkwalk, a table looks much like this.

```
RFC1213-MIB::ipNetToMediaIfIndex.1.203.0.113.1 = INTEGER: 1
RFC1213-MIB::ipNetToMediaIfIndex.1.203.0.113.65 = INTEGER: 1
RFC1213-MIB::ipNetToMediaIfIndex.1.203.0.113.207 = INTEGER: 1
RFC1213-MIB::ipNetToMediaPhysAddress.1.203.0.113.1 =
     Hex-STRING: B8 69 F4 E8 39 0A
RFC1213-MIB::ipNetToMediaPhysAddress.1.203.0.113.65 =
     Hex-STRING: 24 05 0F F6 AE 0D
RFC1213-MIB::ipNetToMediaPhysAddress.1.203.0.113.207 =
     Hex-STRING: 08 00 27 B7 06 A6
RFC1213-MIB::ipNetToMediaNetAddress.1.203.0.113.1 =
     IpAddress: 203.0.113.1
RFC1213-MIB::ipNetToMediaNetAddress.1.203.0.113.65 =
     IpAddress: 203.0.113.65
RFC1213-MIB::ipNetToMediaNetAddress.1.203.0.113.207 =
     IpAddress: 203.0.113.207
RFC1213-MIB::ipNetToMediaType.1.203.0.113.1 =
     INTEGER: other(1)
RFC1213-MIB::ipNetToMediaType.1.203.0.113.65 =
     INTEGER: other(1)
RFC1213-MIB::ipNetToMediaType.1.203.0.113.207 =
     INTEGER: other(1)
```

An SNMP table is a like any other table or spreadsheet, but presented on a column-by-column basis. Our sample here is built on the MIB RFC1213-MIB, used for managing IP-based networks. Each column is named after the object.

The first three lines, all beginning with RFC1213-MIB-::ipNetToMediaIfIndex, are the first column of the table. Every object beginning with this OID is part of the column. The column is named ipNetToMediaIfIndex.

The three lines beginning with a different OID, RFC1213-MIB-::ipNetToMediaPhysAddress, are the second column. Each object's value is set to a hex string. Finally, our last three lines are the column `ipNetToMediaType`.

You'll quickly learn to recognize an SNMP table when you see it in a walk, but viewing it as a table requires the table name. Find table names by reading the associated MIB file (Chapter 4). If you're looking at walk output and don't feel like reading the MIB file, it's a really good guess that the table name is part of the OID. Take the examples above, with OIDs like `RFC1213-MIB::ipNetToMediaType` and `RFC1213-MIB::ipNetToMediaNetAddress`. Discard the MIB name and look at the common elements in what remains. All of these start with `ipNetToMedia`, so try that as a table name.

```
$ snmptable proxy3 ipNetToMedia
SNMP table: RFC1213-MIB::ipNetToMediaTable

Index ipNetToMediaPhysAddress ipNetToMediaNetAddress ipNetToMediaType
    1    "B8 69 F4 E8 39 0A "          203.0.113.1          other
    1    "24 05 0F F6 AE 0D "          203.0.113.65         other
    1    "08 00 27 B7 06 A6 "          203.0.113.207        other
   ...
```

This spits out a three column table. The first line tells us that the table's proper name is `ipNetToMediaTable`, not the "ipNetToMedia" that we typed, but snmptable took a guess at what we wanted and we got lucky.

I'm using this table as an example because it's one of the few that's narrow enough to print in a book. Most tables are far too wide to show on an average terminal. If this book says to run a command on your terminal and follow along, please broaden your terminal and do so.

If snmptable asks "is that a table?" try adding "Table" to your table name. Or search the MIB file (Chapter 4) for the word "table."

You must have the MIB file for the table for snmptable(1) to function. If you don't have the MIB file and try to call a table by numerical OID, snmptable will ask if it's a table.

Modifying and Interpreting Tables

The various net-snmp commands share a whole bunch of command-line flags and arguments. This is great for consistency, but means commands need a way to differentiate their own arguments from those used by other SNMP commands. Snmptable uses the program-specific -C flag to manipulate table display.

Let's consider another table, diskIOTable. It displays disk read and write information. The column headers are all the last parts of the object names: diskIODevice, diskIOReads, and so on. We know that this table is called diskIO; we really don't need to have that part of the name reprinted as a table header. Use -Cb to strip away repeated parts of the column headings. In my particular example, this reduces the table width enough to get the entire table into a standard 80-character screen on a newly booted CentOS machine.

```
$ snmptable -Cb centostest diskIOTable
SNMP table: UCD-DISKIO-MIB::diskIOTable
```

Index	Device	NRead	NWritten	Reads	Writes	LA1	LA5	LA15	NReadX	NWrittenX
1	sr0	0	0	0	0	0	0	0	0	0
2	sda	106533888	6867456	5599	197	0	0	0	106533888	6867456
3	sda1	6270976	2097152	1834	4	0	0	0	6270976	2097152
4	sda2	98681856	4770304	3735	172	0	0	0	98681856	4770304
5	dm-0	94254080	4770304	3567	212	0	0	0	94254080	4770304
6	dm-1	2256896	0	88	0	0	0	0	2256896	0

This is compact enough to display, read, and understand.

The column headers are the unique part of OID names. If you look through the SNMP walk you took this from, you'll see that these represent OIDs like UCD-DISKIO-MIB::diskIOIndex, UCD-DISKIO-MIB::diskIODevice, UCD-DISKIO-MIB-::diskIONRead, and so on.

Each row represents a specific device. This table has a convenient numerical index. Row 1 is sr0, row 2 is sda, row 3 is sda1, and so on. Combine the index with the OID name to see which exact OID the value came from. If you have trouble, search your snmpbulkwalk output on the device for the table header, grab the full OID, and use `snmptranslate -Td` to get the formal definition.

Suppose I'm interested in the number of reads performed on the hard drive. The *NRead* column represents `UCD-DISKIO-MIB-::diskIONRead`, but snmptranslate tells me this is the number of *bytes* read from disk since boot. I don't want bytes read, I want read accesses. The *Reads* column is for `UCD-DISKIO-MIB::diskI-OReads`, which snmptranslate tells me is the number of read accesses since boot. This is my target OID.

The sr device is a Linux CD drive, while the dm devices are device mappers. Line 2, sda, represents the actual hard drive in this host. I combine this with the OID name to get `UCD-DISKIO-MIB-::diskIOReads.2`. I can get the number of disk accesses since boot by querying this specific OID, as we'll discuss later this chapter.

Index Consistency

Add interfaces or storage devices to a host, and you'll add rows to the related SNMP table. Some agents deliberately retain old index values, adding new entries at the end of the table. Others insert a new row in the middle of the table, shifting all the later entries down. When you remove an interface or storage device, that row gets removed from the table. Should the agent keep the same index value on the remaining devices, and leave a blank row in the middle of the table? Or should it shift everything up one?

Whenever you reconfigure a device, check the related tables for an index change. You might need to update your network management system. Most network management systems have specific features to manage index changes for you.

Some vendors let you choose how they behave.

Text Indexes

Not all tables have a column just for indexes. Each of the disk devices in the `diskIO` table has a unique name. Why not just use the device name as an index? Eventually, folks started doing that.

87

You'll see examples of this even with net-snmp. There's a table for interfaces, `ifXTable`, that includes a numerical index that gets mapped to an interface. (There's also an primordial interface table, `ifTable`, that only has 32-bit counters and hence overflows very quickly on modern interfaces. Start off right, use `ifXTable`.)

This is most obvious in routing tables. Every host has a routing table, not just routers. Run `snmptable localhost inetCidrRoute` and you'll grab the local host's routing table in excruciating detail. Go search your snmpbulkwalk for inetCidrRoute, and you'll see OIDs like `IP-FORWARD-MIB::inetCidrRouteIfIndex.ipv4."0.0.0.0".0.3.0.0.1.ipv4."203.0.113.1"`. IPv6 OIDs are even longer. (The quoted parts of the OID are where the manager commands have translated the IP addresses from the hexadecimal used on the wire.) Making the index part of the OID reduces the size of the table and gives a clear object for a specific configuration detail.

The snmptable command doesn't parse index values out of OIDs by default, however. It was written when the table's first column was always the index. Running `snmptable localhost inetCidrRoute` therefore produces a routing table without any indexes, making it useless. Plus, there's an `ifIndex` column that might mislead some folks[12] into thinking there's an index. Add the `-Ci` option to have snmptable parse the index out of the OID. I'd also add `-Cb` to shorten the headers.

```
$ snmptable -Cbi localhost inetCidrRoute
```

You can now see the routing table *with* the routes.

Many objects have "display hints" telling SNMP commands how to display the object's value. When these display hints are not present, net-snmp takes its best guess. Often that guess isn't good enough. If the results in a column look like garbage, it might be displaying the data incorrectly. Use the `-Oa` option to force displaying strings as

---

12   Not saying this was me. *Some* folks. Which could, possibly, include me. In theory.

ASCII, which might help you decipher what the data's supposed to be. Use -Ob to force displaying OID indexes as numbers, which is especially helpful with IP addresses. We'll see an example in Chapter 4.

Further Table Transformations

While -Cb compacts many tables enough to display on a terminal, snmptable supports other output transformations for special circumstances, and even options for querying agents that only support SNMPv1.

Tell snmptable the width of your display with the -Cw option. Here I set the display to 60 characters wide. This will break the table across multiple lines. I'll also add -C's i option, so that snmptable prints the index in the front of every line.

```
$ snmptable -Cibw 60 proxy3 diskIO
SNMP table: UCD-DISKIO-MIB::diskIOTable
```

index	Index	Device	NRead	NWritten	Reads	Writes	LA1	LA5
1	1	sr0	0	0	0	0	0	0
2	2	sda	106533888	7332352	5599	246	0	0

...

```
SNMP table UCD-DISKIO-MIB::diskIOTable, part 2
```

index	LA15	NReadX	NWrittenX
1	0	0	0
2	0	106533888	7332352

...

If you want to feed the output of snmptable to another program, you can transform the output to simplify parsing. The -CH flag removes the column header, while -Cf permits you to specify a delimiter instead of spaces. Here I print a comma-delimited table without the header.

```
$ snmptable -Cf , -CH proxy3 diskIO
2,sda,106533888,7686656,5599,316,0,0,0,106533888,7686656
...
```

Some delimiters, like the pipe symbol, require quoting.

If you are querying an SNMPv1-only device, use -CB to tell snmptable to use only GETNEXT requests rather than GETBULK.

89

Showing Specific Columns

The good news about SNMP is that it exposes almost everything about a host. The bad news is, it exposes more than your mind or your terminal can manage. While the disk I/O table is pretty straightforward, a standard host's network interface table has twenty-two columns. Some of them you won't care about.

Fortunately, Unix originated as an operating system for manipulating text, and those tools remain in the system. Here I use awk(1) to print only columns 2, 5, and 6 from snmptable's output, and column(1) to format them nicely.

```
$ snmptable proxy3 diskio | awk '{print $2,$5,$6}' \
    | column -t
diskIODevice  diskIOReads  diskIOWrites
ada0          47035        45656
cd0           5            0
pass0         0            0
pass1         0            0
```

For a table with a whole bunch of entries, figure out which columns contain data you care about and only show those. Here I examine the very broad `ifXTable` on my test lab router, and print only the columns representing packets in and out. You'll get chopped-up table name information on the first line, which you can ignore.

```
$ snmptable -Cb gwtest ifXTable | \
    awk '{print $1,$6,$10}' | column -t
...
Name         HCInOctets    HCOutOctets
ether1-out   444273014300  156503801442
ether2       0             0
ether3       157651932380  426995610275
ether4       23446252999   3502532925
ether5       238272721     1905516146...
```

Whatever the problem is with my router, every interface but `ether2` is passing packets.

Converting Table Entries to OIDs

So you've looked at a table and found a cell you want to monitor. How do you convert a column and row into an OID?

First, note the index of the entry you want. You might need to use −Ci to show the index in the snmptable output.

The column name is a group of objects in the table. Do an snmp-bulkwalk on the table name, or perhaps even the column name. Find the row of the column you want to monitor. Copy the OID.

That's it. You're done.

Querying Specific Objects

So you've trawled through the SNMP walk of your host and found some stuff you'd like to more specifically check. Grab single objects with snmpget(1).

You only need two arguments to run snmpget, the agent hostname and the object's OID. Suppose you previously found the number of read accesses since boot on a host's hard drive is at the OID UCD-DISKIO-MIB::diskIOReads.2. Give the agent and OID as an argument to snmpget(1).

```
$ snmpget www2 UCD-DISKIO-MIB::diskIOReads.2
UCD-DISKIO-MIB::diskIOReads.2 = Counter32: 6579
```

This host has had 6,579 read requests since boot.

Entering Incomplete OIDs

Entering UCD-DISKIO-MIB::diskIOReads.2 at the command line gets old quick. Many OIDs can be queried by the object name, or the OID name without the MIB name or the colons. The manager will search its MIB files for that short name, and if it finds it, will run the query. Groups and table names are examples of short name. The manager will perform a simple search for matching text, so you must verify that the object returned is the one you hoped for.

91

Here, I ditch the `UCD-DISKIO-MIB` part of the OID and try using only `diskIOWrites.2`.

```
$ snmpget www2 diskIOWrites.2
UCD-DISKIO-MIB::diskIOWrites.2 = Counter32: 3313
```

These short names can be used to identify subsets of the MIB tree. There are several OIDs under `diskIOWrites`. You could even shorten the name further, so long as it remains unique. Here I grab all of the OIDs under `UCD-DISKIO-MIB::diskIOWrites`, using a very truncated name.

```
$ snmpbulkwalk www2 diskIOW
UCD-DISKIO-MIB::diskIOWrites.1 = Counter32: 0
UCD-DISKIO-MIB::diskIOWrites.2 = Counter32: 3322
UCD-DISKIO-MIB::diskIOWrites.3 = Counter32: 4
UCD-DISKIO-MIB::diskIOWrites.4 = Counter32: 2600
UCD-DISKIO-MIB::diskIOWrites.5 = Counter32: 2889
UCD-DISKIO-MIB::diskIOWrites.6 = Counter32: 0
```

You must spell out the full word if you're grabbing a particular child OID, however. Trying to do a GET on `diskIOW.2` fails; you must use `diskIOWrites.2`.

This permits a whole bunch of convenient shortcuts. The enterprise MIB, `.1.3.6.1.4.1`, is available under `enterprises`, letting you scan these MIBs with:

```
$ snmpbulkwalk host enterprises
```

If a particular command on your Unix doesn't allow you to use shortened OID names, enable them with the `-IR` flag. You can also use `-Ib` to search out OIDs by regular expression. Learn about other input modifiers in snmpcmd(1).

Modifying Output

Getting a full line of output is perfectly fine at the command line, but you'd probably need to massage this result to get it into your monitoring system. Net-snmp includes various output modifiers that let you tweak how it presents the result of any query. You can set these on the command line with the −o argument followed by another flag or, if you want them permanently, set them in *snmp.conf*. We'll demonstrate these with snmpget(1), but they also work with other managers like snmpbulkwalk(1).

When you're exploring a system, you might want the response to include either the full formal OID definition in all its polysyllabic glory, or the numerical definition. Use −On, as in "Interpreting OIDs" earlier this chapter, to print OIDs as numbers. Make this permanent by enabling *printNumericOids* in *snmp.conf*.

```
$ snmpget -On proxy3 UCD-DISKIO-MIB::diskIOReads.2
.1.3.6.1.4.1.2021.13.15.1.1.5.2 = Counter32: 6580
```

If you'd prefer to see .iso.org.dod.internet.private. enterprises.ucdavis.ucdExperimental.ucdDiskIO-MIB.diskIOTable.diskIOEntry.diskIOReads.2, use the −Of flag or set the *snmp.conf* option *oidOutputFormat* to 3.

When you query an object, snmpget retrieves its type information from the MIB and displays it with the response. In our example, the type is *Counter32*. Remove that information with −OQ. To remove the type information and the equals sign, use −Oq. You can enable the *quickPrinting* *snmp.conf* option to emulate −Oq, but there is no equivalent to −OQ.

```
$ snmpget -Oq db1 UCD-DISKIO-MIB::diskIOReads.2
UCD-DISKIO-MIB::diskIOReads.2 6580
```

Maybe you just want snmpget to print the answer, not the OID. Use −Ov, or the *printValueOnly* *snmp.conf* option.

```
$ snmpget -Ov db1 UCD-DISKIO-MIB::diskIOReads.2
Counter32: 6580
```

If you're using this in a script, you know what this OID is and you know its type. You just want to check the value and process it somehow. Use −Oqv (or all three corresponding *snmp.conf* options) to get a naked value.

```
$ snmpget -Oqv db1 UCD-DISKIO-MIB::diskIOReads.2
6580
```

Some OIDs in our walk appear perfectly sensible, until you think about them too much.

```
…
IF-MIB::ifOperStatus.1 = INTEGER: up(1)
…
```

This OID shows if network interface number 1 is working. The MIB says that this OID reports an integer, and the SNMP walk shows that integer is *up*. When I went to school, my poor teacher went to a great deal of trouble to persuade me that "up" was not an integer. What's going on?

The MIB file defines 1 as "up," and the command conveniently reminds you of that in the output. You can use -Oe or *printNumericEnums* to skip the reminder, or -Oeqv to return only the number.

```
$ snmpget -Oeqv db1 IF-MIB::ifOperStatus.1
1
```

If you're using `snmp.conf` settings to change the default output format, you can restore the default with -OS.

Net-snmp includes a few other output transformations, but these are the most useful. Read the snmpcmd(1) man page for the complete, current list.

Get Multiple Objects

The snmpget(1) command dates from SNMPv1. If you want to query a whole bunch of objects, you must specify each OID. If you know exactly which objects you want, you can specify the OIDs on the command line.

```
$ snmpget www1 sysORID.1 sysORID.2 \
    sysORID.3 sysORID.4 sysORID.5
```

To grab ranges of objects, though, look at snmpbulkget(1). Despite the name, snmpbulkget is a super-powered GETNEXT client. GET-NEXT does not retrieve the OID you give it, but the OID after the one you give it. Give snmpbulkget(1) an OID, and it retrieves the ten objects *after* that OID.

I most often use snmpbulkget to retrieve table columns. Each OID in the column has an index value somehow attached to it. The column name without the index is before the column name with any index. Consider `diskIOTable` again. The column `diskIOReads` has four entries, ending in .1 through .4. If I want all of those entries, I ask for the column name without any indexes.

Run snmpbulkget just as you would snmpget(1).

```
$ snmpbulkget www1 UCD-DISKIO-MIB::diskIOReads
UCD-DISKIO-MIB::diskIOReads.1 = Counter32: 83058
UCD-DISKIO-MIB::diskIOReads.2 = Counter32: 6580
...
```

Retrieving ten objects is only a default setting. Earlier snmpbulk-walks showed that this host has four disk devices. If I'm monitoring disk reads, what I really want is the four objects for those disks. The *repeaters* characteristic tells a bulk get how many objects to request. Set the number of repeaters with −Cr. Don't leave a space between the option and the number.

```
$ snmpbulkget -Cr4 www1 diskIOReads
UCD-DISKIO-MIB::diskIOReads.1 = Counter32: 83058
UCD-DISKIO-MIB::diskIOReads.2 = Counter32: 6580
UCD-DISKIO-MIB::diskIOReads.3 = Counter32: 0
UCD-DISKIO-MIB::diskIOReads.4 = Counter32: 0
$
```

I can massage this output using any of the snmpget output modifiers in the previous section, arranging them optimally for my monitoring system.

You can retrieve multiple objects with snmpbulkget by listing them on the command line. Suppose you want to monitor both disk reads and writes.

```
$ snmpbulkget -Cr4 www1 diskIOReads diskIOWrites
UCD-DISKIO-MIB::diskIOReads.1 = Counter32: 83058
UCD-DISKIO-MIB::diskIOWrites.1 = Counter32: 4756
UCD-DISKIO-MIB::diskIOReads.2 = Counter32: 6580
UCD-DISKIO-MIB::diskIOWrites.2 = Counter32: 0
...
```

Bulk requests can return any desired combination of objects.

Non-Repeaters

A *non-repeater* is an object that you don't want snmpbulkwalk to repeat. Suppose you want to monitor system uptime along with reads and writes. Uptime, `DISMAN-EVENT-MIB::sysUpTimeInstance`, is a single object. You'd query uptime as a non-repeater, and the other objects as repeaters. The snmpbulkget program can query both simultaneously.

Set the number of non-repeaters with snmpbulkwalk's `-Cn` flag. Here, I set the number of non-repeaters to 2 and retrieve the uptime object as well as `UDP-MIB::udpNoPorts`.

```
$ snmpbulkget -Cn2 proxy3 sysUpTime udpNoPorts
DISMAN-EVENT-MIB::sysUpTimeInstance =
        Timeticks: (994132) 2:45:41.32
UDP-MIB::udpNoPorts.0 = Counter32: 1639
```

I declared I had two non-repeaters. I queried two OIDs. I got two objects back.

You can combine repeating and non-repeating queries in a single command. First, give the number of repeaters and non-repeaters. Put the non-repeating OIDs first, then the repeating queries.

Here I query two non-repeaters and four repeaters. The two non-repeaters appear first, `sysUpTime` and `udpNoPorts`. The remaining OIDs, `diskIOReads` and `diskIOWrites`, each return the four OIDs that follow those requested.

```
$ snmpbulkget -Cn2 -Cr4 proxy3 \
    sysUpTime udpNoPorts diskIOReads diskIOWrites
```

I collected ten objects in a single request, sending one packet and getting only one in return.

If you increase repeaters too high, the response will arrive in multiple packet fragment. If your network is struggling, don't make the problems worse. I find forty repeaters is about the most you can reliably fit in a single packet, but it might be lower for large objects.

Avoid network management systems that rely on individual GETs rather than supporting GETBULK. The offenders don't document this behavior, so you must use a packet sniffer or investigate public discussions.

Timeouts and Retries

SNMP traditionally runs over UDP, which provides no transport-level guarantee of message delivery. Adding a delivery guarantee to SNMP would complicate the protocol. Instead, managers set a timeout on each request, and retry if that request isn't answered.

Timeouts and retry periods vary by product, but they're usually at least one second. Some devices crash when they receive more than one GET per second. Net-snmp uses a one second timeout and retries failed requests up to five times unless something answers.

When your network suffers congestion or other problems, you must make adjustments.

Certain devices need longer timeouts to handle particular requests. Suppose you're telling a router to download a new operating system image from a remote server. Should the router reply to that request when it receives the command and starts copying the file, or should it respond when it finishes the download? Either answer is wrong for a certain subset of users. A slow link between the router and the download server might demand a longer timeout. A device might need extra time to answer a query any other agent answers instantly. These problems are entirely vendor- and network-dependent, and can only be discovered through ~~suffering~~ experience and research. When you have packet loss, add retries.

Adjust net-snmp's timeout with the -t option or the *timeout* snmp.conf keyword. If your network suffers from high latency, increasing the timeout gives the SNMP request a chance to travel and return. Timeouts less than one second, while possible, can crash agents.

The *retries* snmp.conf keyword and the -r command-line flag let you set the number of times the manager resends a command once the timeout expires. It defaults to 5. Note that this isn't the number of times it tries, but the times it retries after the initial attempt. Changing the number of retries is useful on a network suffering from packet loss. With one try and five retries, and a one-second timeout, a net-snmp manager will spend six seconds trying to get a response from a device before giving up.

Suppose you're trying to query interfaces on the router **pnakotic**, on the far side of an overloaded link, to see how much traffic is going through it. You need to walk the OIDs IF-MIB::ifInOctets and IF-MIB::ifOutOctets. There's so much latency that you can't get a response in one second, so increase it to two with -t.

```
$ snmpbulkwalk -t 2 pnakotic IF-MIB::ifInOctets
```

If it turns out that the link is not only congested, it's suffering packet loss, you might need to up the retries as well.

```
$ snmpbulkwalk -t 2 -r 10 pnakotic IF-MIB::ifInOctets
```

When things are going badly, increasing timeouts and retries might let you sneak an SNMP command through to a struggling router to close a flooded interface and preserve the rest of the network.

More Manager Options

Managers have evolved with SNMP. Most managers have features to support many of the protocol's oddities, vendor bugs, and other weirdness. When a manager behaves weirdly with a particular agent, check the documentation and vendor support to see if you must flip a particular toggle for this combination of equipment.

For net-snmp, the snmpcmd(1) manual page lists many but not all of the options all manager programs share, and the separate manager manuals list many more. Not all options are documented in the man pages, however. To view all configuration file options, run the program with the -H flag.

```
$ snmpget -H
Configuration directives understood:
  In snmp.conf and snmp.local.conf:
    alias                     NAME TRANSPORT_DEFINITION
    doDebugging               (1|0)
    debugTokens               token[,token...]
...
```

If you find yourself stumbling into a weird edge case, remember that SNMP has been around a long time and that someone has almost certainly experienced your edge before now. Check the available options and the Internet to see if there's anything relevant. Play with it and see what happens.

Command Line Option Precedence

Having all these *snmp.conf* options is nice, but sometimes you'll need one of those options as a one-off. You can use configuration file keywords as command line options, by prefacing them with a double dash.

Some options have an equivalent command-line single-dash option. The *timeout* keyword sets the length of time for an SNMP query to time out. The default, five seconds, is plenty for almost all cases. There's a -t command-line flag to let you set a timeout on the fly. You could also set it on the command line as --timeout.

Many of these have a catch, though. Unlike most other software, the configuration file entries might—not always, but *might*—override the command line. If you encounter this, the double-dash version of the command line argument always overrides the configuration file.

Now let's explore MIBs. Don't worry, the tentacles don't bite. Much.

Chapter 4: The Management Information Base

You can now grab individual data points and entire tables of information from an SNMP agent. That's great, so long as you are running net-snmp's managers and agent. When you start looking at devices from other vendors, though, you must find MIB files for those vendors' proprietary MIBs.

Digging through MIB files raises questions, though. Questions that can only be answered by examining the files. Yes, net-snmp and MIB browsers like SnmpB have convenient tools for translating the various forms of the different objects and showing descriptions and parents and whatnot—but nothing can replace reading the comments in the source code or MIB file. Unfortunately.

We'll start by looking at a few MIB files, then cope with collecting and deploying new ones.

MIB Files

A MIB file contains the definitions for a Management Information Base. That sounds easy, but people somehow manage to regularly muck it up. We expect MIB files to be named after the MIB they define: that is, `IF-MIB` should be defined in a file named *IF-MIB*. Certain operating systems indicate file types with filename suffixes, however, so these files become *IF-MIB.txt*, and that convention bled into other operating systems. Other folks decided that while MIB files were written in plain text, they had a specific purpose, so they use the extension *.mib* or *.my* instead. Still other organizations decided that if SNMP had been a pain to implement it should be a pain to use, and so created their own indecipherable naming standard.

Having "one MIB per file" is a tradition, not a requirement. Some vendors will define multiple MIBs in a single file named after the vendor or the best-known MIB. Most big networking companies have devoured many smaller firms during their endless reigns, and the condemned souls who serve in their support departments would much rather tell people to install one big file SHOGGOTH-MIB as opposed to dozens of files named after each of the firm's many meals—er, *acquisitions*.

Unfortunately, many people have programmed their prejudices about MIB file names into their SNMP tools. Some tools expect all files to end in .mib, .txt, or .my. Others expect exactly one and only one MIB per file. If your network management system somehow chokes on MIB files, double-check the software's expectations. Don't blame the NMS if it won't import an invalid MIB file.

Perhaps the most common error sysadmins make is conflating the MIB file with the MIB. The MIB file on the manager is a reference for the actual MIB as implemented in the agent.[13] If you have inexplicable errors when querying, remember that the two things are separate and reconsider your problem.

Net-snmp includes a selection of sixty-odd common MIB files defining core SNMP MIBs and a few net-snmp enterprise MIBs. It won't translate any enterprise MIBs, but you should be fine with general snmpbulkwalks against most agents. The packages install the MIB files in a location like /usr/local/share/snmp/mibs/ or /usr/share/snmp/mibs/.

If you're running Debian, you must download the standard MIB files with the snmp-mib-downloader package. Debian requires all software and files included in the base system to be freely modifiable and redistributable. MIB files are standards documents, and not free by Debian's definition. This makes sense—we need the actual MIB files as defined in the standard, not a version some well-meaning person "fixed" to fit what they thought was correct.

---

13   The map is not the territory. The unwholesome grimoire is not the unspeakable entity it summons.

Reading MIB Files

Most readers of this book should never need to write a MIB file, unless you're writing code to implement an enterprise MIB for your software. You do need to know how to glean basic information from MIB files, however.

MIB files use a very strict syntax, defined by SMI-2. The syntax has been updated over time, so files that were compliant in 1987 might not be completely so today. Also, vendors exhibit different levels of care about errors in their MIB files. Between the two, you'll see syntax variations everywhere.

Take a look at *SNMPv2-MIB.txt*.

```
SNMPv2-MIB DEFINITIONS ::= BEGIN

IMPORTS
  MODULE-IDENTITY, OBJECT-TYPE, NOTIFICATION-TYPE,
  TimeTicks, Counter32, snmpModules, mib-2
    FROM SNMPv2-SMI
    ...
```

All MIB files start with a formal declaration identifying what they're defining. This file defines something called SNMPv2-MIB. It then imports data type definitions like MODULE-IDENTITY, OB-JECT-TYPE, NOTIFICATION-TYPE, timeticks, Counter32, snmp-Modules, and mib-2 from a MIB called SNMPv2-SMI.

Below that you'll see the MODULE-IDENTITY section that tells you who's responsible for this version of this MIB. It usually includes the date of the last update and the contact information for the authors. The date information, as defined in LAST-UPDATED, is especially useful if you suspect you have an outdated MIB. Some MIBs use VERSION rather than LAST-UPDATED. In theory, these values always increase. The manager software doesn't use these fields, but provides them for your edification and troubleshooting. While net-snmp takes care to ensure all the MIBs it includes are up to date, third party collections might be less scrupulous.

After that, we get the DESCRIPTION.

```
...
DESCRIPTION
    "The MIB module for SNMP entities.

    Copyright (C) The Internet Society (2002). This
    version of this MIB module is part of RFC 3418;
    see the RFC itself for full legal notices.
...
```

What I find most important here is the standards document (RFC) that defines this version of this MIB. If I have any questions on how to interpret an object defined in SNMPv2-MIB, I can refer to RFC 3418.

Below that I might find revision information, giving the dates of previous versions and the defining RFCs. This particular MIB was revised three times after its publication on 1 April 1993.[14]

Then the MIB file begins to define the MIB tree and individual objects within that tree. Any lines beginning with a double dash (--) are comments. They might contain valuable hints, or just declare that something went obsolete thirty years ago and you should never encounter it.

```
...
-- the System group
--
-- a collection of objects common to all managed
    systems.
system    OBJECT IDENTIFIER ::= { mib-2 1 }
```

This defines a single object. It's called `system`. The OBJECT IDENTI-FIER is a mandatory field where we'd normally see information about the OID, but it contains nothing. The `::=` statement is an assignment, giving it its full OID value and declaring where it attaches to the rest of the MIB tree. Remember how the full name of the average OID starts with `iso.org.dod.internet.mgmt.mib-2`? This "system" OID is `.1` beneath `mib-2`. If you search through the MIB files, you'll find that *SNMPv2-SMI.txt* defines `mib-2`, along with `mgmt`, `internet`, `dod`, `org`, and `iso`.

---

14   April Fool's Day is the best day for unspeakable acts. By the time people realize you're not joking, it's too late.

This is perhaps the simplest useful object definition. It doesn't exist to provide information, but only to hold other objects. (You'll also see these types of entries to assign labels to sub-OIDs.) We've seen the `system` group at the top of every snmpbulkwalk; it includes items like operating system, uptime, and other really common characteristics. Let's look at another entry.

```
sysDescr OBJECT-TYPE
    SYNTAX        DisplayString (SIZE (0..255))
    MAX-ACCESS    read-only
    STATUS        current
    DESCRIPTION
        "A textual description of the entity.  This value
        should include the full name and version identi-
        fication of the system's hardware type, software
        operating-system, and networking software."
    ::= { system 1 }
```

This defines the object `sysDescr`. Look down at the bottom of the definition, with the `::=` sign. This is `system.1`, or `iso.org.dod.internet.mgmt.mib2.system.1`. Going back to the definition, we see that it appears as a string of 0 to 255 characters. It's read-only, and current (so it's not obsolete). The DESCRIPTION tells us this object contains a description of the host. Return to your snmpbulkwalk output and look at the `sysDescr` object.

```
SNMPv2-MIB::sysDescr.0 = STRING: Linux
    centos.blackhelicopters.org 3.10.0-1062.1.1.el7.x86_64
    #1 SMP Fri Sep 13 22:55:44 UTC 2019 x86_64
```

That's a fair description of this host. The .0 at the end indicates that this object won't have children or siblings: it's a scalar value, a leaf, complete in itself, as defined in the MIB.

The rest of the MIB file contains more definitions, explicit group assignments, and potentially illuminating comments. Some comments point to RFCs other than the one used to define the MIB as a whole, which give more details or context on individual objects. Also, searching for "Table" shows tables supported by the MIB. That doesn't mean that a random agent supports all those tables, but it's worth running snmptable(1) against your agents to see if it summons anything intriguing. All MIB files end with an END statement.

Compiling MIBs

When a manager reads a MIB file, it pulls in other MIB files by reference. Using the MIB file demands having those required MIB files. Your manager *compiles* its MIB files to try to resolve the dependencies between them and build a single view of its global MIB.

Your manager can only interpret and translate MIBs that it has all of the MIB files for. While net-snmp ships with all the common MIB files for the SNMPv2 MIB, enterprise MIBs are trickier. If MIB file A requires MIB file B, and B requires C, you need all three. Your manager can still walk the MIB tree and report numbers, but it can't provide any interpretation of the results without all the necessary MIB files.

Work with SNMP for any length of time, and you'll have to dig up more MIB files.

Additional MIB Files

The default MIB files work great so long as you never leave the cozy shelter of the base SNMP standards. The moment you want to interrogate agents on other operating systems or networking devices, though, you'll need the MIB files that document the MIBs implemented on those agents. This task has three parts: identifying which MIBs you need definition files for, finding those MIB files, and telling net-snmp to read and use the MIB file.

Do not add your newly discovered MIB files to the directory where your manager puts its default MIB files, unless you actively desire chthonic misery. Upgrades might overwrite that directory. MIB files from different organizations might conflict. You want a good collection of MIB files at hand, but not where your manager will automatically read all of them. We'll discuss why in "Net-SNMP and MIB Files" later this chapter.

Use snmpbulkwalk(1) to find which MIBs an agent supports. I'm choosing to poke at my spare router, **gwtest**. First walk the main OID tree, then check the enterprise tree. Save the results.

```
$ snmpbulkwalk gwtest > gwtest.walk
$ snmpbulkwalk gwtest enterprise > gwtest.enterprise
```

Scan both files for sections of the tree that are missing object names and descriptions of the values. Here's a snippet of the standard snmpbulkwalk.

```
...
IPV6-MIB::ipv6AddrStatus.11.' ...............' = INTEGER: preferred(1)
IPV6-MIB::ipv6AddrStatus.11.'.........i....9.' = INTEGER: preferred(1)
SNMPv2-SMI::mib-2.9999.1.1.1.1.0 = STRING: "MikroTik DHCP server"
SNMPv2-SMI::mib-2.9999.1.1.1.2.0 =
        OID: MIKROTIK-MIB::mikrotikExperimentalModule
SNMPv2-SMI::mib-2.9999.1.1.6.4.1.4.192.168.1.2 = INTEGER: 1
SNMPv2-SMI::mib-2.9999.1.1.6.4.1.4.203.0.113.51 = INTEGER: 2
...
```

The stuff starting with IPv6-MIB might disturb those not illuminated by IPv6 understanding, but it's clear that net-snmp knows what these OIDs represent. The output suddenly switches to a bunch of numerical OIDs when it hits SNMPv2-SMI::mib-2.9999. Net-snmp knows about SNMPv2-SMI, and mib-2, but it has no idea what the 9999 beneath mib-2 represents.

The Internet Assigned Numbers Authority (IANA) maintains a public list of enterprise MIB assignments at https://www.iana.org/assignments/enterprise-numbers/enterprise-numbers. This index isn't necessarily helpful, though. 9999 is assigned to an organization or person that has no apparent relationship with Mikrotik. This isn't uncommon; the contact is often "the poor schlub assigned to that project that week."

Fortunately, the Internet is full of MIB indexes. An Internet search for SNMPv2-SMI::mib-2.9999 quickly reveals that the MIB DHCP-SERVER often uses this. It's based on a standards draft from 2004 that was never accepted, due to patent concerns. While IANA has not officially assigned that OID to DHCP management, a whole bunch of vendors use it anyway.[15]

Checking the snmpbulkwalk for the enterprise objects, and performing Internet searches on those OIDs, reveals that we need MIB files for `SNMPv2-SMI::enterprises.9` (Cisco Systems), `SNMPv2-SMI::enterprises.3495` (National Laboratory for Applied Network Research), and `SNMPv2-SMI::enterprises.14988` (MikroTik).

Knowing who owns these OID numbers is helpful, but how do we find the actual MIB files? The four sources are, in order of preference: the vendor, MIB file collections, scrounging for MIB files, and stripping the standard. The order of the last two varies depending on which method has most recently burned me.

Vendor MIBs

Equipment vendors usually have files for their enterprise MIBs on their web site. You might have to hunt a bit to get all of the needed files. The good news is, vendor MIB collections are usually up to date. Mostly. Maybe the files on their web site aren't up to date, but the support department has those files. Hopefully.

Of the four OIDs on our list, Cisco and Mikrotik offer MIB files on their sites. Mikrotik offers their single file, while Cisco's main FTP server offers dozens of MIB files and a tarball containing all of them.

When in doubt, pillage a vendor's MIB files. Take them all. Leave no survivors. You won't need all of them, but compiling your desired vendor MIB file probably requires one or more additional vendor MIB files.

MIB File Collections

For decades, I kept a great big tarball of MIB files I had painfully gleaned from the chaff of the Internet. Don't do that. The easiest way to gather a bunch of MIB files is to make other people do the work

---

15   This sentence contains everything you need to know about vendors' desire to comply with standards and other people's patents.

for you. Searching the Internet uncovers several great collections of MIB files. My favorite is from the Netdisco project, available at https://github.com/netdisco/netdisco-mibs. Here I download that collection.

```
$ cd .snmp/mibs
$ git clone https://github.com/netdisco/netdisco-mibs
```

In a few moments, I'll have a stash of 4500 popular MIB files that other people have both found useful and performed some amount of sanity-checking on. This collection contains the Mikrotik MIB file, as well as many but not all Cisco MIB files. Fetching the originals from the vendor was worthwhile.

These collections are maintained on a best effort basis by volunteers, to meet their own needs. I hesitate to recommend any particular collection, because today's excellent resource is tomorrow's open sewer. These folks provide valuable services on a best-effort basis. Many of these collectors don't have the equipment needed to test all of their MIB files, so the quality of such collections varies. I applaud their work, but who knows what malarial Internet swamp they originally found the file on? Plus: is the reference site still maintained? Do they update the MIB files when new ones are discovered? Is the entire site an insidious practical joke meant to drive hapless sysadmins to perceive things they were not meant to know?

My best suggestion is to use collections that appear curated by someone who does similar work to you. I'll trust a network administrator's router MIB collection, but maybe not their Unix MIBs.

While a bad MIB file can't really hurt your agents, at least with read-only queries, it makes interpreting objects challenging. The MIB files I've downloaded from vendors were on occasion optimized for customer misery, but they most often aren't actively *incorrect*. Some are, if the vendor is particularly lazy, careless, or ignorant. MIB files from third parties lack even that unreliable guarantee.

If you encounter a bad MIB file in a collection, let the site maintainer know. Politely. Remember, they run such sites as volunteers. The horror imposed on you by a bogus MIB file is nothing compared to the nightmares they experience every time they work on their site.

Scrounging for MIB Files

Some MIB files are not so easy to find. Maybe they were created by a vendor that went out of business in a distant millennium, or they were eaten by a giant megacorp and their MIBs live on only as assimilated code inside their agents. Or maybe they were written by some doofus author who provides his bibliography at **snmp.mwl.io** via the **megadweeb** community as a lame gag, and you can only get the MIB file from the book's entry on his web site.

Various folks have built OID reference sites, describing who owns what enterprise MIBs in convenient web pages that let you download individual MIB files. These sites have all the problems of MIB collections, but are easier to peruse.

Sometimes, you can't find any better source for a MIB file than what's on such a site. Download what you can find and consider the results nothing more than hints from a dubious informant: worth investigating, but not actionable without careful verification.

If you have trouble finding a MIB using an OID like `SN-MPv2-SMI::enterprises.3495`, try using the fully numerical version instead, in this case `.1.3.6.1.4.1.3495`. I spent quite some time searching for this particular MIB file using the mixed name, but once I used the numerical version `SQUID-MIB` came right up. With this hint, I went straight to the Squid web site and grabbed the official MIB file.

Sometimes a scrounged MIB file flat-out doesn't work. You can use a tool like smilint(1) to see if there's anything you can twiddle to fix it, but most of us are better off scrounging for a different version of the MIB file.

Debian created the snmp-mibs-download tool specifically to help scrounge for MIB files. If you're not running Debian, the source code for this program contains a bunch of hints on where to look for MIB files.

Stripping Standards Docs

After searching and scrounging, you have what look like the correct MIB files. But maybe you've found multiple different MIB files that claim to authoritatively represent a particular enterprise MIB. Or you've found an old standard document for a MIB, but all the MIB files you've found for it are incoherent.

If you look at an RFC, or an Internet Draft for a proposed RFC, you might notice that they're written in a strictly formatted style. It's so strictly formatted that it's possible to programmatically rip the MIB file out of the standard with smistrip(1). It's not part of the usual net-snmp packages, but most Unixes have a package that includes it.

First, find the latest version of the standard you can get your hands on. I'll use the never-approved DHCP MIB, `SNMPv2-SMI::-mib-2.9999`, for my example. My Internet searches tell me that the last, unapproved proposal was *draft-ietf-dhc-server-mib-10.txt*. I find a copy of this document in plain text format, download it, and run smistrip against it.

```
$ smistrip draft-ietf-dhc-server-mib-10.txt
DHCP-SERVER-MIB: 1287 lines.
```

I now have a file *DHCP-SERVER-MIB*. That was easy.

Using it, now. That's a whole different bucket of tentacles.

Net-SNMP and MIB Files

Your host has a collection of MIB files, managed either by the package manager or an add-on tool like Debian's `download-mibs` from the snmp-mibs-download package. Find out which directory by using the `--default-mibdirs` option to net-snmp-config(1).

```
$ net-snmp-config --default-mibdirs
/home/mwl/.snmp/mibs:/usr/local/share/snmp/mibs
```

Your host manages the system MIB directory, something under */usr*. Don't add your collection of MIB files to that directory; you'll muck up the package. Instead, use the $HOME/.snmp/mibs directory provided for exactly this.

To use new MIB files, first decide how to manage MIB files. You can tell net-snmp to read all of the files in a directory, requiring you to move files around the filesystem when you want the SNMP commands to not parse certain files. Alternately, you could dump all your MIB files in a single directory and give net-snmp a list of MIBs to read. Which is better depends entirely on your sysadmin preferences. I prefer reading an entire directory, as I carefully select which MIBs to read.

Make your choice using the *mibs* snmp.conf option, the *MIBS* environment variable, or the -m option to any snmp command. The configuration file sets a default, the environment variable overrides the configuration file, and the command line overrides everything. I'll use the *mibs* snmp.conf value as an example, though you could set it in any of the three methods. Here I set *mibs* to all.

```
mibs            all
```

If you want to tell net-snmp the names of specific MIBs to read from MIB files, start by running net-snmp-config --default-mibs to view the initial list.

```
$ net-snmp-config --default-mibs
:SNMPv2-MIB:IF-MIB:IP-MIB:TCP-MIB:UDP-MIB:
HOST-RESOURCES-MIB:NOTIFICATION-LOG-MIB:
DISMAN-EVENT-MIB:DISMAN-SCHEDULE-MIB:
HOST-RESOURCES-TYPES:MTA-MIB:
...
```

The default MIB list usually includes everything shipped with net-snmp, though your Unix might change the list. This is not a list of files to read: it's a list of MIB definitions within MIB files. Remember, some vendors will dump multiple MIBs into one file. It's colon-delimited, and the list both ends and starts with a colon.

To add MIBs to the list, set them as a colon-delimited list in *mibs* in snmp.conf. To add your MIBs to the beginning of the list, put a minus sign (-) at the beginning of the list. To add your MIBs to the end of the list, put a plus sign (+) at the beginning. If you list neither a plus nor a minus sign, your list completely replaces the built-in MIB list. That's probably[16] not what you want. If multiple MIBs conflict, the first MIB listed wins.

Adding Single MIB Files

Suppose I want to add my router vendor's MIB, SHOGGOTH-MIB to the list, plus the SQUID-MIB that I scrounged off a disreputable web site. Set it in *snmp.conf* as so.

```
mibs +:SQUID-MIB:SHOGGOTH-MIB:
```

I could also set this as an environment variable, overriding the default setting.

```
$ MIBS=+:SQUID-MIB:SHOGGOTH-MIB: ; export MIBS
```

To use a specific MIB on a particular command run, I could set this at the command line.

```
$ MIBS=+:MIKROTIK-MIB:SHOGGOTH-MIB:DAGON-MIB: ; export MIBS
```

Or I could override all existing settings with the −m command-line flag.

```
$ snmpbulkwalk -m +SHOGGOTH-MIB mainrouter enterprise
```

Such overrides are less of an issue on modern hardware, unless you're using a Raspberry Pi as a remote monitoring node. For most interactive, interrogative use, setting MIBS to all suffices.

Don't Load All The MIB Files

As sysadmins, we want *all* the knowledge. The natural instinct would be to have net-snmp know about every single MIB file you own. This way lies madness.

Every time you run a net-snmp manager command, it compiles (loads, parses, and resolves dependencies) every MIB file. All this loading and parsing slows your commands. Plus, each time you run a

---

16   Some vendors insist that they own the universe, however. Or, at least, own you.

command it rediscovers every error in every file. Some of those errors are bad enough that they spew to your screen. Some of the files you've found will do nothing but spew errors. Repeated exposure to MIB parsing errors will destroy any lingering faith you might have had that humanity deserves to exist.

Additionally, some MIB files conflict with each other. MIB files from one vendor might define a term for that vendor's use. That's fine, until another vendor happens to use that same word for its definitions. Errors will abound. If you have enough MIB files, conflicts are inevitable.

Don't automatically stick every single MIB file you find in `$HOME/.snmp/mibs`. Exercise discretion as you curate your MIB collection. Sometimes, though, discretion and curation are insufficient. You might find you need an entirely different collection of MIB files for different devices.

Adding MIB Directories

Asking multiple users to maintain separate copies of identical MIB files is bogus. You shouldn't add MIB files to the package-managed directories. Additionally, if you're unlucky enough to use vendors that write conflicting MIB files, you might need to use an entirely different collection of MIB files to examine those devices. You might well want a central collection of necessary MIBs, maintained and updated by the sysadmins and shared by all users. Add directories by setting a colon-delimited list with the *mibdirs* `snmp.conf` option, the MIBDIRS environment variable, and/or the -M command-line flag.

To add the new directories to the end of the directory list, start it with a plus sign. To begin the list with your choices, start the list with a minus sign. If you don't list either, your list overrides the default MIB directories. Suppose you have a collection of MIB files in `/usr/local/snmpmibs/`. To add these to the default directories via `/etc/snmp/snmp.conf`, use the *mibdirs* option. Start the list with a plus sign to search these MIBs last.

```
mibdirs +/usr/local/snmpmibs/
```

Set the MIBDIRS environment variable to override this list for a particular user or session.

To change the MIB directory on a single command, use the -M command-line option and the directory. This is useful when you must select a collection of MIB files to examine a particular device.

```
$ snmpbulkwalk -M +:/usr/local/mibs/shoggothcorp/ -m ALL router13
```

MIB files in directories later in the list override those in earlier directories. If multiple MIB files in different directories define the same MIB, the directory listed last takes precedence.

Testing MIB Files

To verify a MIB file works with your manager, stare the problem in the face and walk that part of the SNMP tree. I want to see if the DH-CP-SERVER MIB file I extracted from the expired standard returns useful results. I copy the file *DHCP-SERVER-MIB* to *$HOME/.snmp/mibs* and run snmpbulkwalk against my lab's test router.

```
$ snmpbulkwalk gwtest SNMPv2-SMI::mib-2.9999
DHCP-SERVER-MIB::dhcpv4ServerSystemDescr.0 =
      STRING: MikroTik DHCP server
DHCP-SERVER-MIB::dhcpv4ServerSystemObjectID.0 =
      OID: MIKROTIK-MIB::mikrotikExperimentalModule
DHCP-SERVER-MIB::dhcpv4ServerClientLeaseType.'....' =
      INTEGER: static(1)
DHCP-SERVER-MIB::dhcpv4ServerClientLeaseType.'..q3' =
      INTEGER: dynamic(2)
DHCP-SERVER-MIB::dhcpv4ServerClientLeaseType.'..q5' =
      INTEGER: dynamic(2)
DHCP-SERVER-MIB::dhcpv4ServerClientLeaseType.'..q6' =
      INTEGER: dynamic(2)
...
```

This looks suspiciously like an SNMP table. Digging through the MIB file uncovers several tables. The most immediately interesting is the dhcpv4ServerClientTable, which supposedly lists the hardware and IP addresses of all DHCP clients. The output is far too wide to fit on a screen, let alone this book, so I'll chop it down to displaying only the first, fifth, and eighth columns. I use the -Cb flag to show brief column headers, and -Ci to include the index extracted from the OID.

```
$ snmptable -Cbi gwtest dhcpv4serverclienttable | \
      awk '{print $1,$5,$8}' | column -t
index      TimeRemaining  PhysicalAddress
'....'     305            1,6,88:4a:ea:44:1:d2
'..q3'     315            1,6,a4:da:22:2f:69:e7
'..q5'     564            1,6,b4:74:43:62:a3:91
```

Okay, this resembles something that sort of makes sense. Sort of. The TimeRemaining column is in minutes, according to the MIB file, and PhysicalAddress is a MAC address. But what the heck is the value in the index? I don't know anything about hosts called ..q3, and I would expect an IP address somewhere in this table.

As discussed in Chapter 3, managers use the Textual Convention and Display-Hint parameters to determine how to show values. If the MIB defines no Display-Hint for an object, the manager takes its best guess. Here, that best guess is wrong. Use the -Ob flag to say "don't try to display this index as a word, show it numerically."

```
$ snmptable -Ob -Cbi gwtest dhcpv4serverclienttable | \
      awk '{print $1,$5,$8}' | column -t
index          TimeRemaining  PhysicalAddress
203.0.113.51   520            1,6,a4:da:22:2f:69:e7
203.0.113.53   460            1,6,b4:74:43:62:a3:91
203.0.113.54   410            1,6,b8:e9:37:2a:5:30
...
```

We get a list of IP addresses, and the hardware addresses they're assigned to. The leading 1,6 indicates these are Ethernet addresses.

Resolving MIB Dependencies

In addition to the simpler Squid, DHCP, and Mikrotik MIB files, we downloaded the entire dumpster of Cisco MIB files. Those are the sort of thing you'll want to keep on hand, but copying every single MIB file into $HOME/.snmp/mibs will generate errors. Copying something like the entire netdisco MIB file collection into your `mibs` directory makes the different vendor MIBs squabble for control of your manager and spills hundreds of lines of outrage across your screen. On the other tentacle, MIB files have dependencies. How can you select the needed MIB files?

Most of these collections are curated to resolve dependencies together. You can use each collection as a discrete entity, swapping them out en masse as needed. But maybe you need a single collection with the most essential MIBs. How do you achieve that?

Start with the most specific OID you want to manage. I grabbed the Cisco MIB files to see what my test router was reporting at SN-MPv2-SMI::enterprises.9.9.150.1.1.1.0. An Internet search shows this is part of CISCO-AAA-SESSION-MIB. Find the file defining that MIB and copy it to your MIB file directory.

Now let's give your manager what it needs to resolve the dependencies in this MIB file. Search your new MIB file for an OBJECT-TYPE entry. It doesn't matter what that entry is, or if it's supported on your agent. I grabbed the first I could find from the Cisco MIB file, `casnActiveTableEntries`.

```
…
casnActiveTableEntries OBJECT-TYPE
        SYNTAX        Gauge32
        MAX-ACCESS    read-only
…
```

Now use snmptranslate on this OID. Use the -m command-line argument to forcibly read this MIB file into this command. Add -Td to request a translation and explication of this OID. Using -IR tells an SNMP command to search the MIB for a short OID name. Give the name of your chosen OID.

```
$ snmptranslate -m CISCO-AAA-SESSION-MIB -Td -IR \
      casnActiveTableEntries
MIB search path: /home/mwl/.snmp/mibs:/usr/local/share/snmp/mibs
Cannot find module (CISCO-SMI): At line 33 in
      /home/mwl/.snmp/mibs/CISCO-AAA-SESSION-MIB.my
Did not find 'ciscoMgmt' in module #-1
      (/home/mwl/.snmp/mibs/CISCO-AAA-SESSION-MIB.my)
Unlinked OID in CISCO-AAA-SESSION-MIB:
      ciscoAAASessionMIB ::= { ciscoMgmt 150 }
...
```

A few dozen lines of errors informs you that everything immediately imploded. The key phrase you're looking for is "Cannot find module." It's the second line of output, right after the MIB search path. This MIB has a dependency on the MIB CISCO-SMI to compile. Check your hoard of downloaded MIB files, and you'll see the file *CISCO-SMI.my*. There's no guarantee that a file named after a MIB contains that MIB, but it's a good first place to look. Copy the file to your *mibs* directory and try the translation again. If you get a useful answer, you're done. Otherwise, identify the next missing module and grab its file.

Iterate through this for every unidentified OID tree in your agent's MIB, forever.

MIB Errors

Why would MIB files have errors? Maybe the developer didn't want to learn SMI-2, and instead copied from a MIB that they thought was similar to what they wanted to do.

The standards for writing MIB definitions have changed through the decades. Some of those changes conflict with one another. When it comes to SNMP and a minimally viable product, some vendors believe that the word "viable" means "it works so long as nobody pokes it too hard." MIB files have errors.

Also, MIB definitions can reserve keywords. While some vendors work to make certain their MIBs are internally consistent, they're less considerate about cooperating with other vendors. Otherwise useful and helpful MIB files misbehave when competing MIBs rip away their definitions.

More than one vendor ships a MIB file that includes everything you need to compile the MIB. What would normally be in multiple files is one giant file. That helps with their products, but when you have devices from multiple vendors you wind up with multiple definitions for the roots of the MIB tree—and of course, rather than stick with the standards, vendors can't help making minor tweaks to the parent MIBs to make them conform to their prejudices.[17] Not only do individual MIB files have errors, your particular combination of MIB files generates unique errors.

Whenever the MIB files in use do not compile properly, net-snmp responds by telling you where it's looking for MIB files.

```
$ snmpbulkwalk proxy3
MIB search path: /home/mwl/.snmp/mibs:/usr/share/snmp/
mibs:/etc/snmp/mibs
...
```

As it walks through the MIB files, it prints out each error it finds, in order.

```
...
Cannot find module (DLINK-SWPRIMGMT-MIB): At line 61 in
        /etc/snmp/mibs/des3018-l2mgmt.mib
Did not find 'des3018' in module #-1
        (/etc/snmp/mibs/des3018-l2mgmt.mib)
Unlinked OID in DES3018-L2MGMT-MIB:
        swL2MgmtMIB ::= { des3018 2 }
...
```

You've got a few different ways to handle these errors: fix, avoid, or ignore.

Yes, mere mortals can fix MIB files. You could use a tool like smilint(1) to analyze a MIB file and refer to the standards to polish it. If you're using a MIB file for an open source project and delving into the alien geometries of SMI-2 interests you, there's no reason you shouldn't give it a shot. The -Pw and -PW flags show increasing details on MIB parsing errors. Errors that involve conflicts with other MIB files aren't

---

17 Some standards are outdated, so I can't blame vendors—no, wait, yes I *can* blame them. And do. If a 20th-century standard doesn't work today, update it properly so we can all continue to work together. That's what the Internet is for.

exactly hopeless, but require one provider or another to change. You should never, under any circumstances, attempt to fix a commercial vendor's MIB file; despite what they'd like you to believe, never forget that if you pay for their product, they work for you. If you do successfully fix it, you'll need to repeat your work at the next firmware version.

Avoiding such errors means altering how you handle MIB files. Maybe a MIB file runs error-free on its own, but as soon as you add it to the list of MIBs to be processed both it and other MIB files show errors. This is when you consider creating separate directories for MIB files from different vendors and using -M on the command line, or manually entering lists of MIBs with -m. What method works best for you?

Why would you ignore errors? Because trash vendors provide equally trash MIB files. You can't fix them. You can't avoid them. The High Priest of Finance won't let you melt down the equipment or trebuchet it into the Sun. You must endure the errors. You can at least send the errors off to some place you never have to see. The -Lf (Chapter 6) flag lets you set a destination for errors. You could set this to a log file you'll never look at, but I find it useful to send unwanted and unsolvable errors somewhere they'll never trouble me.

```
$ snmpbulkwalk -Lf /dev/null proxy3
```

There is no configuration file option to set this permanently. You might consider using a shell alias. Sometimes those errors explain the garbage you see in the report, though, so maybe don't.

Examining MIBs

Working with SNMP will quickly acquaint you with the industry-standard MIB tree. All these enterprise MIBs have their own features and hierarchy, though. How can you learn the MIB, short of cracking open the MIB file and studying the arcane contents? The snmptranslate(1) program includes an assortment of features for examining MIB files. We've already seen `snmptranslate -Td`, for printing the definition of an object behind an OID.

You can also perform regular expression searches on the compiled MIBs, by using the -TB option. I use this most often when I encounter an interesting object and want to see any objects that might be related. Here I search for OIDs that include "vacm."

```
$ snmptranslate -TB vacm
SNMP-VIEW-BASED-ACM-MIB::vacmMIBConformance
SNMP-VIEW-BASED-ACM-MIB::vacmMIBGroups
SNMP-VIEW-BASED-ACM-MIB::vacmBasicGroup
...
```

Chapter 9 discusses VACM.

If you want to see how your MIB fits together, try printing the entire MIB in tree form with the -Tp flag. To show only a part of the tree, give the OID as an argument. Here I generate a graph of the SQUID-MIB that caused so much annoyance earlier this chapter.

```
$ snmptranslate -Tp 1.3.6.1.4.1.3495
+--nlanr(3495)
   |
   +--squid(1)
      |
      +--cacheSystem(1)
      |  |
      |  +-- -R-- Integer32 cacheSysVMsize(1)
      |  +-- -R-- Integer32 cacheSysStorage(2)
      |  |
      |  +--cacheUptime(3)
      |
...
```

If the tree is too wide for your screen, add the -w flag and desired width in characters.

```
$ snmptranslate -Tp -w 80 1.3.6.1.4.1.3495
```

Studying the MIB tree can be illuminating, although darkness has much to recommend it.

Writing scripts that read objects in the MIB and transform the output is often easiest when you can produce the MIB in a certain form. The -Ta flag spills out the MIB with only the OBJECT IDEN-TIFIER information, so you could feed it to a script and generate your own tree view. Using -Tl generates a list of OIDs with both name and number. The -To flag dumps a list of numerical OIDs in the MIB, while -Ts dumps the MIB by names.

All of these commands compile the entire MIB. That can be unde-sirable, especially if you're trying to figure out where two MIB files ar-gue with each other or you're just sick of that one MIB file's insolence. Use the -m and -M flags to examine select MIBs or select directories of MIB files, plus any parents automatically pulled in. Here I want a tree of one particular vendor's MIB file. I want it printed 80 characters wide, and I want to start showing the tree at the enterprise MIB of .1.3.6.1.4.1. I must specify the start OID numerically.

```
$ snmptranslate -Tp -m DAGON-MIB -w 80 .1.3.6.1.4.1
```

Could I do this by specifying the top of the vendor's enterprise OID instead? Uh… sort of. Specifying the vendor's OID would show me anything under the vendor's OID, but not anything the MIB file tried to sneak in elsewhere in the MIB. Not that your vendors would ever be tricky or nefarious, of course.

If you suspect the vendor has snuck stuff into the agent outside their reserved enterprise OID, have snmptranslate show the tree from the root of .1. The tree will be wider, but you'll almost always find un-expected details.

```
$ snmptranslate -Tp -m DAGON-MIB -w 80 .1
```

You are now prepared to cope with MIB files. As prepared as any mortal can be, at least.

Chapter 5: The Net-SNMP Agent

The net-snmp agent, snmpd(8), provides information about a host to an SNMP manager. Configured properly (or improperly, depending on your perspective), it can offer managers remote control capabilities. We'll cover basic configuration and its impact on the system in this chapter. Later chapters will delve into specific agent configurations as appropriate for the topic.

My most common issue configuring snmpd is that it doesn't refuse to start when the configuration file contains unknown configuration keywords. If you make a typo in a configuration option, the agent will restart just fine. The new setting won't work, but the agent will run. There is no option to validate the entire configuration file. Whenever you have a problem, check the log file and double-check the configuration options.

Configuring snmpd(8)

We added a few user accounts and communities to `snmpd.conf` in Chapter 2, the minimum needed to support querying a private test host. Now we're going to discard that minimal configuration and set up a more full-featured agent that looks something like what you'd see in the real world. Net-snmp provides a handy tool for setting up snmpd: snmpconf(1).

Scripted Configuration

We used snmpconf(1) in Chapter 1 to demonstrate aggregating net-snmp configuration files. Now we'll set up an agent configuration more like what you'd use in the real world. Go to a directory that doesn't normally host snmp configuration files, such as `/tmp` or `$HOME`, and use the `-g basic_setup` option.

```
$ snmpconf -g basic_setup
The following installed configuration files were found:

    1:   /home/mwl/.snmp/snmp.conf
    2:   /etc/snmp/snmp.conf
    3:   /etc/snmp/snmpd.conf

Would you like me to read them in?  Their content will
be merged with the output files created by this session.
Valid answer examples: "all", "none","3","1,2,5"
Read in which (default = all): none
```

Here, snmpconf has scanned the host for existing configuration files. Reading in existing configuration files is quite handy when you want to use snmpconf to update an existing configuration or amalgamate several configuration files into a single cyclopean entity. Note that the persistent data file, /var/net-snmp/snmpd.conf, is missing from the list. Creating a new snmpd configuration doesn't touch the persistent data file, so it retains previously created SNMPv3 users, interface indexes, and other agent metadata.

We're creating a wholly new configuration, so don't read in any existing files.

```
*******************************************************
*** Beginning basic system information setup ***
*******************************************************
Do you want to configure the information returned in the
system MIB group (contact info, etc)? (default = y): y
```

That is the point of what we're doing, so enter y.

You'll then see a series of questions, complete with explanatory text.

```
Configuring: syslocation
Description:
  The [typically physical] location of the system.
    Note that setting this value here means that when
    trying to perform an snmp SET operation to the
    sysLocation.0 variable will make the agent return
    the "notWritable" error code.  IE, including this
    token in the snmpd.conf file will disable write ac-
    cess to the variable.
```

124

```
  arguments:  location_string
```
The location of the system: **MWL global datacenter**

Finished Output: syslocation "MWL global datacenter"

The "Configuring" keyword at the top of the question gives you the configuration file option you're setting here. Here, we're setting the *syslocation* keyword. The "Description" tells us this is where the host resides. We also get a warning that if the location is hard-coded in `snmpd.conf`, we won't be able to change it via SNMP later. I'm setting the location to "MWL global datacenter."[18] The last line shows us the `snmpd.conf` entry created by our answer.

```
Configuring: syscontact
Description:
  The contact information for the administrator
    Note that setting this value here means that when
    trying to perform an snmp SET operation to the
    sysContact.0 variable will make the agent return
    the "notWritable" error code.  IE, including this
    token in the snmpd.conf file will disable write ac-
    cess to the variable.
    arguments:  contact_string
```
The contact information: **mwl@mwl.io**

Finished Output: syscontact mwl@mwl.io

This similar question lets you set the email address via the *syscontact* keyword. Someone who queries this SNMP agent can contact the system owner for more information. It might not be vital in your lab, but in an enterprise it's vital.

Then we get something very different.

```
Do you want to properly set the value of the
sysServices.0 OID (if you don't know, just say no)?
(default = y): y
```

---

18   It's my datacenter. I keep a globe in it, ergo: a global datacenter. Globes are way cool. Mine shows the USSR.

```
Configuring: sysservices
Description:
  The proper value for the sysServices object.
    arguments:  sysservices_number
```

The sysservices configuration option is a number that indicates the type of services the host provides, as per RFC 3418. If you're using SNMP to manage telecom systems, this number is vital; for those of us who provision IP-based services, less so. We don't need to know the specifics of that calculation, however, as `snmpconf` has a handy tool to calculate it for us.

```
does this host offer physical services (eg, like a
     repeater) [answer 0 or 1]: 0
does this host offer datalink/subnetwork services
     (eg, like a bridge): 0
```

Our average test server is not a repeater or a bridge. Answer 0.

```
does this host offer internet services (eg, supports IP): 1
does this host offer end-to-end services (eg, supports TCP): 1
does this host offer application services (eg, supports SMTP): 1
```

The whole purpose of a server is to offer TCP/IP services. Answer all of these with 1. You'll get a convenient answer with the *sysservices* keyword.

```
Finished Output: sysservices 76
```

If you ever write your own *snmpd.conf* for servers, you could recycle this value across them all. Hosts that are repeaters or bridges, or that support IP but don't offer any services on it, need different values.

```
********************************************
*** BEGINNING ACCESS CONTROL SETUP ***
********************************************
Do you want to configure the agent's access control?
(default = y): y
```

"Access control" means communities and SNMPv3 users. This will not create new users, merely set the *rwuser* and *rouser* statements that created users to access the agent.

```
Do you want to allow SNMPv3 read-write user based access
     (default = y): y
```

A "read-write user" is a user with read and write access. We intended the user **secureRW** for that purpose, so let's grant it access.

```
Configuring: rwuser
Description:
   a SNMPv3 read-write user
      arguments:  user [noauth|auth|priv] [restriction_oid]

The SNMPv3 user that should have read-write access: secureRW
The minimum security level required for that user
      [noauth|auth|priv, default = auth]: priv
The OID that this community should be restricted to
      [if appropriate]:

Finished Output: rwuser  secureRW priv
```

The first line shows us that we're configuring the keyword *rwuser*. We enter the username (**secureRW**) and the desired privacy level (*priv*). We could restrict this user to a subset of the MIB by entering an OID they could query beneath, but let's skip that for now by hitting RETURN. The last line shows the final configuration that gets added to `snmpd.conf`.

```
Do another rwuser line? (default = y): n
Do you want to allow SNMPv3 read-only user based access
      (default = y): y
```

We also created a read-only user **secureRO**. Grant that user read-only access in our new configuration.

```
Configuring: rouser
Description:
   a SNMPv3 read-only user
      arguments: user [noauth|auth|priv][restriction_oid]

Enter the SNMPv3 user that should have read-only access
      to the system: secureRO
The minimum security level required for that user
      [noauth|auth|priv, default = auth]: priv
The OID that this community should be restricted to
      [if appropriate]:

Finished Output: rouser  secureRO priv
```

We're creating a *rouser* statement, as per the first line of this section. The username is **secureRO**, and it requires a minimum privacy level of *priv*. The section ends with showing us the new user. The users created in Chapter 2 now have access to our new configuration.

```
Do you want to allow SNMPv1/v2c read-write community
    access (default = y): n
```

We have SNMPv3, so we don't need communities.

```
*******************************************
*** Beginning trap destination setup ***
*******************************************
Do you want to configure where and if the agent will
send traps? (default = y): n
```

Chapter 12 discusses traps. Skip this for now.

```
*******************************************
*** Beginning monitoring setup ***
*******************************************
Do you want to configure the agent's ability to monitor
various aspects of your system? (default = y): y
Do you want to configure the agents ability to monitor
processes? (default = y): y
```

Monitoring is one of an agent's main functions. When the manager queries the agent for a monitoring object, the agent checks the host. If the host is in a state that the agent is configured to call an error—say, there's too many processes, or the disk is too full—the agent sets the object's value to an error as defined in the MIB.

Start by monitoring processes.

```
Configuring: proc
Description:
  Check for processes that should be running.
    proc NAME [MAX=0] [MIN=0]

    NAME:  the name of the process to check for.  It
    must match exactly (ie, http will not find httpd
    processes).
    MAX:   the maximum number allowed to be running.
    Defaults to 0.
    MIN:   the minimum number to be running.  Defaults
    to 0.
```

```
The results are reported in the prTable section of
the UCD-SNMP-MIB tree
Special Case:  When the min and max numbers are both
0, it assumes you want a max of infinity and a min of
1.
```

Snmpd monitors processes by exact name, using the *proc* keyword
and setting an upper and lower bound on the number of that process
that should be running at any given time. Each proc line monitors one
process name. We start by monitoring cron (crond in some Unixes).
One and only one cron process should be running at any moment.

```
Name of the process you want to check on: cron
Maximum number of processes named 'cron' that should be
      running [default = 0]: 1
Minimum number of processes named 'cron' that should be
      running [default = 0]: 1
Finished Output: proc  cron 1 1
Do another proc line? (default = y): y
```

When the program asks if I want another proc line, I must decide
if I want to monitor more processes. I do, so I answer y. I want to
monitor php-fpm. I need at least one php-fpm running, but no more
than ten.

```
Maximum number of processes named 'php-fpm' that should
      be running [default = 0]: 10
Minimum number of processes named 'php-fpm' that should
      be running [default = 0]: 1
Finished Output: proc  php-fpm 10 1
```

Finally, let's monitor sendmail. It should be absent most of the
time, but if it runs amok something's decidedly wrong.

```
Name of the process you want to check on: sendmail
Maximum number of processes named 'sendmail' that should
      be running [default = 0]: 10
Minimum number of processes named 'sendmail' that should
      be running [default = 0]:
Finished Output: proc  sendmail 10
Do another proc line? (default = y): n
```

I'm done with process monitoring, so when asked if I want to add
another proc line I say n.

Those three cases suffice to serve as examples for Chapter 11, on monitoring.

```
Do another proc line? (default = y): n
Do you want to configure the agents ability to monitor
    disk space? (default = y): y
```

We're finished with processes, for now. Let's monitor some disk partitions with the *disk* keyword. Depending on your operating system and how you installed it, you might or might not have partitions other than root (/) on disk. Here I tell snmpd to verify that /tmp is at least 10% free.

```
Configuring: disk
Description:
  Check for disk space usage of a partition.
    The agent can check the amount of available disk
    space, and make sure it is above a set limit.

  disk PATH [MIN=100000]

  PATH:   mount path to the disk in question.
  MIN:    Disks with space below this value will have
  the Mib's errorFlag set. Can be a raw integer value
  (units of kB) or a percentage followed by the %
  symbol.  Default value = 100000.


  The results are reported in the dskTable section of
  the UCD-SNMP-MIB tree
Enter the mount point for the disk partion to be checked
    on: /tmp/
Enter the minimum amount of space that should be
    available on /tmp/: 10%

Finished Output: disk  /tmp/ 10%
Do another disk line? (default = y): y
```

I'll repeat this for the root partition, but I'm deliberately telling it to alarm when the partition is 1% full. We'll use this as an example in Chapter 11.

```
Enter the mount point for the disk partion to be checked
    on: /
Enter the minimum amount of space that should be
    available on /: 99%

Finished Output: disk  / 99%
Do another disk line? (default = y): n
```

Next, snmpconf offers to alarm at chosen load levels for you, with the *load* keyword.

```
Do you want to configure the agents ability to monitor
    load average? (default = y): y
```

Monitoring load average is extremely system-dependent, especially in this age of innumerable tiny virtual machines scurrying around like rats in the walls. But we're here to learn, so let's set it up.

```
Configuring: load
Description:
    Check for unreasonable load average values. Watch the
    load average levels on the machine.

    load [1MAX=12.0] [5MAX=12.0] [15MAX=12.0]

    1MAX:   If the 1 minute load average is above this
    limit at query
    time, the errorFlag will be set.
    5MAX:   Similar, but for 5 min average.
    15MAX:  Similar, but for 15 min average.

    The results are reported in the laTable section of
    the UCD-SNMP-MIB tree

Enter the maximum allowable value for the 1 minute load
    average: 10
Enter the maximum allowable value for the 5 minute load
    average: 8
Enter the maximum allowable value for the 15 minute load
    average: 5
```

Heavy but brief computing loads are less interesting than less heavy but longer-running loads. I don't want an alarm for a short spike unless it's a *big* spike. I set the load limits at 10, 8, and 5.

```
Do another load line? (default = y): n
Do you want to configure the agents ability to monitor
     file sizes? (default = y): y
```

One load monitoring entry is plenty. Let's watch the size of a few files, with the files keyword. The files available depend on your Unix, so I'm picking a couple of not-uncommon examples. For our tests, use files that exist on your system. First, I monitor /var/log/messages to make sure it stays less than 1 GB. This option only accepts file sizes in kilobytes, so you must do some math. One gigabyte is 1,048,576 kilobytes.

```
Configuring: file
Description:
   Check on the size of a file.
      Display a files size statistics. If it grows to be
      too large, report an error about it.

      file /path/to/file [maxsize_in_kilobytes]

   if maxsize is not specified, assume only size
   reporting is needed.

   The results are reported in the fileTable section of
   the UCD-SNMP-MIB tree
Enter the path to the file you wish to monitor:
     /var/log/messages
Enter the maximum size (in kilobytes) allowable for
     /var/log/messages: 1048576
Finished Output: file  /var/log/messages 1g
Do another file line? (default = y): y
```

Here I make a second file entry for another log file. This file should never be above 5 KB in size.

```
…
Enter the path to the file you wish to monitor:
     /var/log/secure
Enter the maximum size (in kilobytes) allowable for
     /var/log/secure: 5

Finished Output: file  /var/log/secure 5
Do another file line? (default = y): n
```

Two files will do for now.

Once we finish configuring file monitoring, net-snmp writes the file and exits.

```
...
The following files were created:

  snmpd.conf
...
```

The snmpconf program tells you where to put the file if you want to use either on the system as a whole, or only in your account. The latter isn't useful for *snmpd.conf*, but you could also use snmpconf to create an *snmp.conf* for the various manager programs.

Reviewing snmpd.conf

Take a look at your new *snmpd.conf*. It's not only plain text, it's designed to be easily read.

Hash marks indicate comments. The `snmpconf` program comments the files it creates, mostly using the same text it offered when you made your choices. The uncommented lines are configuration entries, all exactly what snmpconf showed after its "Finished Output" statements.

An *snmpd.conf* configuration statement takes the form of a keyword and one or more arguments, as shown here. Different keywords overwhelmingly represent very different system features, so don't expect them to look alike.

```
...
proc  cron 1 1
disk  /usr/home/ 1g
rwcommunity  insecureRW 203.0.113.0/24
...
```

Copy your new *snmpd.conf* to the location your Unix uses for the primary net-snmp configuration files, probably */etc/snmp/snmpd.conf*. Restart snmpd.

New Agent Functions

Certain net-snmp features don't work unless you configure them. The OIDs do not exist until they are configured. Conveniently, the `snmpd.conf` creation script leaves comments in the file telling you how to check configured features. Most often these are tables.

Now that we've set up process monitoring, query the agent's `prTable` to check those processes.

```
$ snmptable -Cbw 80 proxy3 prTable
SNMP table: UCD-SNMP-MIB::prTable

Index    Names Min Max Count ErrorFlag                 ErrMessage  ErrFix
    1     cron   1   1     1  noError                               noError
    2  php-fpm   1  10     0    error No php-fpm process running noError
    3 sendmail   0  10     2  noError                               noError
```

There's an error—php-fpm isn't running! That's okay, because my test host doesn't run PHP-FPM. I monitored it specifically to generate an error. Several examples are like that, so we'd have something to chew on in Chapter 11. Take a look at `dskTable`, `laTable`, and `fileTable`. Everything in those tables is an individual OID that you can monitor separately.

Now let's talk about changing some core agent functions.

Agent Networking

Snmpd defaults to listening on every IPv4 address on the host, on UDP port 161. This industry standard won't work everywhere, however. Use the *agentaddress* `snmpd.conf` keyword to change how the agent attaches to the network. The keyword takes one argument, a colon-delimited list of protocol, address, and port.

`agentaddress` *protocol:host:port*

Configure a UDP port with the *udp* keyword. Here I explicitly configure the default of "UDP port 161 on all IPv4 addresses." I can skip the hostname if it's not needed, but if I specify a protocol I must give a port.

```
agentaddress udp::161
```

Use of *agentaddress* disables the default of listening on all addresses on UDP port 161. If you want that default as well as your custom-configured address or port, you must explicitly state it. Use an additional *agentaddress* keyword to attach to each unique combination of protocols, addresses, and ports. I run a network from this millennium, so I must listen on IPv6 as well as IPv4. Use the *udp6* protocol.

```
agentaddress udp::161
agentaddress udp6::161
```

List particular addresses by hostname or IP address. Remember that using hostnames adds a dependency on name service. Consider your failure paths before imposing any dependency. Here I listen only on **localhost**. I skip the protocol and port, as specifying only an address implies UDP.

```
agentaddress 127.0.0.1
agentaddress ::1
```

If I want to run over both TCP and UDP, use the *tcp* and *tcp6* options. Remember, even if you prefer TCP, best practice is to configure UDP as a fallback.

```
agentaddress tcp::161
agentaddress tcp6::161
agentaddress udp::161
agentaddress udp6::161
```

Changing the agent port is useless for security, but it might help you avoid interfering with a Unix vendor's proprietary agent. Using a sub-agent via AgentX (as Chapter 8 discusses) is preferable, but many vendor agents explicitly refuse to play well with others.[19]

You can also listen on Unix sockets, by using the *unix* keyword and a path to the socket.

```
agentaddress unix:/var/run/net-snmp
```

---

19   The only successful strategy for coping with a jealous unknowable entity is "be somewhere else."

Some combination of *agentaddress* options should make snmpd available on any modern network. If you're trying to connect via something bleeding-edge like DTLS, or something obsolete like IPX, read snmpcmd(1) for more options.

You can specify protocol and port with net-snmp manager programs, as discussed in Chapter 3.

```
$ snmpstatus tcp:router4:1161
```

If you get an answer, you have connectivity.

Agent User

Snmp agents are expected to manage the operating system. They can change the routing table and more. This means they must run with privilege. On a Unix system, that means running as **root**. Running daemons as **root** has long been known as horrible practice, and is responsible for a whole bunch of security breaches. If you're not using the agent to change the host, I encourage you to run the agent as an unprivileged user.

You can run snmpd as a user other than **root**. It won't be able to change the host, but it will provide read access and send traps. You must create a dedicated unprivileged user account and group to run snmpd and own all related files. Don't piggyback on another unprivileged account like the oft-abused **nobody**. The **nobody** account is specifically intended to support NFS, and applying it elsewhere is a gaping security hole. Give your unprivileged user an easily recognizable name, like **snmpd**. The account should have a locked-out shell like /sbin/nologin and a nonexistent home directory. The account that runs a daemon must not own the agent's configuration files.

Once you have a user and group, use the *agentuser* and *agentgroup* keywords to tell snmpd to reduce its privileges to those.

```
agentuser snmpd
agentgroup snmpd
```

The agent starts as **root** so that it can bind to low-numbered network ports, but does all further work as **snmpd**.

Unixes such as Solaris and AIX handle security very differently, using features like capabilities and role-based access control. Consult their documentation for details.

System MIB Configuration

The System group of objects, the very start of the SNMPv2-MIB that appears at the beginning of every snmpbulkwalk, contains vital information about the host. The whole `.1.3.6.1.2.1.1` MIB tree is intended to familiarize the manager with the host. You can configure many of these OIDs in *snmpd.conf*, or you can change them via SNMP commands. You cannot do both. Settings hard-coded in *snmpd.conf* cannot be overridden.

Should you leave these values so they can be configured via SNMP? That's up to you. If you intend to manage a fleet of dynamically-created servers using SNMP, maybe they need to be writable. If your servers are very static, perhaps hard-coding these is better.

Give a system location, as given in `SNMPv2-MIB::sysLocation.0`, with the *syslocation* keyword. Our snmpconf run set it for us.

```
syslocation  "MWL global datacenter"
```

The syscontact keyword declares who is responsible for this system and is displayed in `SNMPv2-MIB::sysContact.0`. Again, snmpconf set it.

```
syscontact  mwl@mwl.io
```

The object `SNMPv2-MIB::sysName.0` gives the hostname. An agent normally runs hostname(1) to retrieve it. You can lie to outsiders by setting `sysName`.

```
sysName nodens.mwl.io
```

The system description, `SNMPv2-MIB::sysDescr.0`, normally comes from running `uname -a`. The standard says that this object should contain the full name and version of the host's operating system as well as information on the type of hardware and networking software. You can add information to this, but don't discard it all in favor of something that describes the system role.

```
sysDescr "mwl's black hole of wasted hope"
```

Don't do this. Many management systems search this object for words they recognize. Always include the operating system and hardware description, even if that description is "virtual machine at the Miskatonic colo."

You now have an agent to freely abuse. Let's help it complain about its suffering.

Chapter 6: Logging

One of Unix's strengths is the multiple channels for data to flow through and the way everything can be plugged into everything else. Net-SNMP takes advantage of these features with support for logging warning and error messages to standard file descriptors, files, and syslogd(8). These options work across the entire suite of programs. You can forward snmpbulkwalk errors to syslog, or snmpd problems to standard out.

Configure logging with the -L command-line option, followed by various flags and modifiers. Just as -C adjusts per-command behavior, -I adjusts how commands handle input, -O handles how programs provide output, and -L manages logging.

We'll start by discussing the standard file descriptors and files, then syslog.

File Descriptors and Files

All Unix programs start with three standard file descriptors: standard input (*stdin*), standard output (*stdout*), and standard error output (*stderr*). In interactive use, net-snmp commands make heavy use of standard out and standard error.

The most authoritative way to discover all the options a net-snmp command supports is to run the command with the -H flag. Many Unix commands have such a function, and when they give pages of information I'll often direct the output to a file for comfortable perusal. Net-snmp prints that help to standard error rather than standard out, however. Standard error is meant for error messages, and while "what you typed is not runnable, try one of these instead" certainly qualifies as an error message, I still want it in a file. You can use assorted shell-dependent tricks to redirect standard error to a file, but the net-snmp suite has a command-line flag to direct output where you need.

The −Le option tells the command to spill any warnings and errors to standard error output. These messages appear on the terminal, mixed in with the regular output, but if you redirect the command's output to a file they remain on the terminal. This is the default for interactive commands. You might use this on the command line to monitor snmpd, though you're better off using snmpd −f to keep snmpd attached to the terminal and enabling debugging with −Dall.

If you want the warnings and errors directed to standard out, mixing them in with the command's normal output, use −Lo. I could have used this with snmpd −H and then redirected the output to a file.

```
$ snmpd -Lo -H > snmpd-options
```

If you want to run snmpd in debugging mode, use −Lo to spill the output to the terminal.

```
# snmpd -f -Dall -Lo
```

The −Lf option, followed by a filename, tells the command to log any warnings to a file. This is the standard for snmpd(8) and snmptrapd(8). Snmpd doesn't use syslog by default; it logs directly to */var/log/snmpd.log*. Examine this file for any warning messages. If you think you're losing errors and warnings in a flood of snmpbulkwalk output, you might send those to a file.

```
$ snmpbulkwalk -Lf /tmp/snmpbulkwalk.messages bigrouter
```

For long term use, you probably want to configure the programs to use syslog(3).

Net-SNMP and Syslogd

Configure net-snmp's syslog support entirely on the command line. There are no configuration file options for logging. Logging is a common net-snmp function: you can log snmpbulkwalk warnings and errors just as easily as messages from snmpd and snmptrapd. You must understand syslog facilities and priorities to configure logging.

Configure syslog by choosing a syslog facility with the -Ls option and a facility. Use d for *daemon* or u for *user*. If you want to use a *local* facility, use the facility number (0-7). Net-snmp supports only the *daemon*, *user*, and assorted *local* facilities. Here I tell snmpd to log to facility *local0*.

```
# snmpd -Ls 0
```

While syslog is most commonly used for daemons, you can also use it in your network management system. Malformed queries waste network and server resources. Adding -Ls0 to your management poller's command line logs these errors so you can track them down in your copious free time.

Most, but not all, messages get *notice* priority.

Priority Selection

Net-snmp assigns all messages and warnings a syslog-style priority. Whether you're using syslog or not, you can filter where you send messages by priority. You could write rules to say "send only critical and above to syslog," or something complicated like "send emergency, alert, and critical messages to standard error, but consign all other messages to the log file." This takes a combination of a command-line flag and a number.

Net-snmp assigns numerical and mnemonic codes to each priority. You'll use the code as a command-line argument to configure logging.

- *emergency* 0 or !
- *alert* 1 or a
- *critical* 2 or c
- *error* 3 or e
- *warning* 4 or w
- *notice* 5 or n
- *information* 6 or i
- *debug* 7 or d

Filtering defaults to sending any messages of the specified or greater priority. Greater priority messages have a lower number. A filter of 4 includes everything with a priority 0-4. Any messages not included in a filter are silently discarded. Specify a range of priorities with a hyphen. The filter 1-3 includes alert, critical, and error messages.

Filtering messages uses the same command line options as redirecting messages, but as a capital letter. Where sending messages to standard out requires -Le, directing messages by priority uses -LE. You'll use -LF to send filtered messages to a file, -LS for syslog, and -LO for standard out. Give the priority immediately after the flag, but before any file or syslog facility.

Here I send all snmpd(8) messages of priority 0 through 4 to standard error. It's an intermediate step between using snmpd -f and normal operation.

```
$ snmpd -LE 4
```

In this snmpbulkwalk command, I send only messages of priority 3-7 to standard error. All other-priority messages are discarded. If I got many error messages, this might help me ignore the minor disasters but view the big horrible problem.

```
$ snmpbulkwalk -LE 3 mainrouter
```

Here I direct messages of priority 0 through 5, as well as priority 7, to standard error. Messages of priority 6 go to the file /tmp/snmpd.options.

```
$ snmpd -H -LE 0-5,7 -LF 6-6 /tmp/snmpd.options
```

If you want to be incomprehensible, mix numerical and alphabetical codes. Long command lines are bad enough without resorting to madness like this.

```
$ snmpd -H -LE 0-n,7 -LF i-6 /tmp/snmpd.options
```

You can now steer net-snmp output any which way you like.

Debugging net-snmp Daemons

I've spent many frustrating hours trying to figure out what snmpd(8) thinks it's doing. The simplest way to figure this out is to run snmpd in debugging mode, with the -D flag. Add -f to keep it in the foreground, and direct the output to your terminal with -Lo.

```
$ snmpd -f -Lo -D
```

This generates piles of output. Fortunately, you can debug snmpd on a module-by-module basis by giving the module name as an argument to -D. We discussed modules at the end of Chapter 1. Here I debug the SNMPv3 user authentication module, *usm*.

```
# snmpd -f -Lo -Dusm
```

When a user tries to authenticate, I get messages like this.

```
...
usm: USM processing completed.
usm: USM processing begun...
usm: Unknown User(secureRX)
```

Someone typo'd their username.

Now let's use SNMP to configure SNMP.

Chapter 7: SNMP SET

Reading information via SNMP is very useful, but what about issuing instructions to the agent? Where's the "management" part of SNMP? SNMP's SET instruction lets you change the value of select objects, which tells the agent to change the host as the object dictates.

How much SETs can do depends on your agent and your vendor. SET is useful but not all-powerful for net-snmp agents on Unix hosts. Many embedded equipment manufacturers, though, let you completely reconfigure their devices via SNMP. There's a whole spectrum between them. I've seen firewalls that make their packet filters accessible with SNMP, routers that let you change routes by SNMP, and more.

Overwhelmingly, vendor-specific functions are under the vendor's enterprise MIB and vary wildly. If you lock yourself out of SSH access on a certain vendor's equipment[20], you can reenable access or even load an entirely new configuration by SNMP. Other vendors let you reboot their gear via enterprise objects, or run scripts pre-loaded onto the device. None of this is something you want to first try in an emergency. Set up your secure users and test the functionality in your lab before going live. No matter what, you must read the vendor documentation very carefully before trying to configure the device with SNMP. Enterprise MIBs vary widely between vendors—that's the point of them, after all—so I won't cover them.

Net-snmp supports SET commands with snmpset(1). Writing objects requires you know the object you want to write, the type of information it uses, and what you want to change it to.

---

20   I won't name names, but in a few centuries someone with a similar name will wind up in charge of a Cardassian-built space station and solidify his reputation as one of Starfleet's great captains.

Writable OIDs

Each object can have certain types of values. We've seen strings, numbers, timeticks, IP addresses, and more. The MIB as implemented in the agent defines the legitimate values for an object, and the MIB should document that.

Every walk against a common agent starts with the OID `SNMPv2-MIB::sysName.0`, the system name. Let's check the definition of that object.

```
$ snmptranslate -Td SNMPv2-MIB::sysName.0
SNMPv2-MIB::sysName.0
sysName OBJECT-TYPE
  -- FROM        SNMPv2-MIB, RFC1213-MIB
  -- TEXTUAL CONVENTION DisplayString
  SYNTAX        OCTET STRING (0..255)
  DISPLAY-HINT  "255a"
  MAX-ACCESS    read-write
  STATUS        current
  DESCRIPTION   "An administratively-assigned name for
  this managed node.  By convention, this is the node's
  fully-qualified domain name.  If the name is unknown,
  the value is the zero-length string."
::= { iso(1) org(3) dod(6) internet(1) mgmt(2) mib-2(1)
      system(1) sysName(5) 0 }
```

So, this object should, but doesn't have to, contain the host's fully qualified domain name. Let's use the OID to grab the system name from my test hosts.

```
$ snmpget -Ov freebsdtest SNMPv2-MIB::sysName.0
STRING: freebsdtest
$ snmpget -Ov centostest SNMPv2-MIB::sysName.0
STRING: centostest
$ snmpget -Ov debiantest SNMPv2-MIB::sysName.0
STRING: debiantest
$ snmpget -Ov gwtest SNMPv2-MIB::sysName.0
STRING: 2019testrouter
```

None of these are incorrect hostnames.[21] The standard claims it

---

21   Yes, the hostname of my test router includes the year I deployed it. I have multiple decades of test gear around the lab. My obituary will include the words "topple" and "crush."

should (not *must*, but *should*) be the host's fully qualified domain name, not the short hostname.

Other agents on my network provide the fully qualified domain name, however. This might not be a big deal in your network. If you're scripting network management, however, inconsistent hostname formats are *deeply* annoying. What format the hostnames appear in probably isn't important, but consistency between hosts is. Everything should report a short hostname, or everything should report the fully qualified domain name.

Let's change these.

Data Types

Each object is limited to certain kinds of data. You'll see responses like strings, IP addresses, integers, and more. We touched on these data types in Chapter 1, but if you want to change an object's value you have to pay attention to it. Fortunately, whenever you do an SNMP GET, by any command, it defaults to telling you the data type. Look at the queries we ran in the last section. Each response is of type STRING.

Setting an object requires specifying the type of data. If you try to set an object to something that doesn't fit the object, you'll get an error. You can't set an integer or IP address to "All Hail Azathoth" or some other string; it won't work.

The snmpset program assigns each data type a one-letter code. You must have the code to set the object. The complete list of codes appears in snmpset(1), but the most common ones are i for Integer, s for String, and a for IP address.

We want to change a string. That'll be type s.

Equipped with this information, we can change the object.

Using snmpset

Use snmpset(1) to set an object. This command takes four arguments: the agent hostname or IP, the OID, the data type code, and the new value.

```
$ snmpset hostname OID typecode new-value
```

Our agents list short hostnames in SNMPv2-MIB::sys-Name.0. This object only accepts strings, type code s. I want to add the complete domain name to this OID.

```
$ snmpset freebsdtest SNMPv2-MIB::sysName.0 s \
       freebsdtest.mwl.io
SNMPv2-MIB::sysName.0 = STRING: freebsdtest.mwl.io
```

The command's output is taken from the agent's response to the manager, so we can be confident the SET worked. If you're not certain, double-check.

```
$ snmpget -Ovq freebsdtest SNMPv2-MIB::sysName.0
freebsdtest.mwl.io
```

The agent has the new hostname!

Changing the agent's hostname across the entire network becomes a matter of hitting the up-arrow key and substituting hostnames.

snmpset Effects

The effectiveness of an snmpset(1) varies depending on how tightly the agent is integrated into the operating system. On some platforms, certain SETs only affect the agent. On platforms that treat SNMP as a first-rate management protocol, the SET affects the underlying operating system. What you have is entirely platform-dependent.

Routers and embedded devices, in general, take SNMP instructions and apply them directly to the operating system. If you change the hostname via SNMP and log into a command line session, the new hostname appears.

On Unix systems, most SETs are isolated to the agent. Each of our reference platforms—CentOS, Debian, and FreeBSD—use a different mechanism to change the hostname, and it all happens in userland. Net-snmp is not so tightly integrated into any of these platforms. When you change the hostname by SNMP, it affects only the agent and not the host. The agent will report the new hostname, but if you run `hostname` at a command prompt you'll get the old hostname. This is not a bad thing, so long as you know it. If I'm sitting at a shell prompt and I type either `ping debiantest` or `ping debiantest.mwl.io`, I get a response. The responses from the agent need merely be consistent with those results. Thanks to the agent's persistent data file, those changes remain after restarting the agent or rebooting the host.

Other object changes directly affect the host. Consider `IP-MIB::ipForwarding`, the object that dictates if a host will forward packets between interfaces. A packet filtering firewall must forward packets, while hosts like web and mail servers don't. When you're upgrading your firewall cluster, you might want to disable packet forwarding on certain nodes so you can work on them. Check the object definition.

```
$ snmptranslate -Td IP-MIB::ipForwarding
IP-MIB::ipForwarding
ipForwarding OBJECT-TYPE
  -- FROM       IP-MIB
  SYNTAX        INTEGER {forwarding(1), notForwarding(2)}
  MAX-ACCESS    read-write
...
```

This object is writeable, according to the MIB file. This doesn't mean that the agent can write the object on this specific host, merely that the MIB permits it. Writing it means changing the value. This object takes an integer, and has two valid values: 1 and 2. Check the current value.

```
$ snmpget -Ov fw1 IP-MIB::ipForwarding.0
INTEGER: forwarding(1)
```

Great. Let's stop it from forwarding. This object uses data type INTEGER, with a code of `i`.

```
$ snmpset fw1 IP-MIB::ipForwarding.0 i 2
RFC1213-MIB::ipForwarding.0 = INTEGER: not-forwarding(2)
```

This router is no longer forwarding packets. The cluster automation should take it out of service. Whether this change will persist past a reboot or not depends entirely on how closely the host is integrated with the agent.

Managing Interfaces with SET

Participating in an enterprise network is about working with other people and managing shared resources. I've lost count of how many times in my sysadmin career the network team has run out of ports on important switches and been forced to recover unused ports.[22] When this happens you must examine your servers to determine which network ports are used and which are plugged in just to make the link light turn on. For a single server you could log in with SSH and check the values, but if you have a whole server farm running Linux, SNMP is a more time-effective and scriptable solution. Interface management is not implemented on all Unixes, so be sure to check.

First, check the interfaces on your host. The interface table ifX-Table has a whole bunch of columns, but we're most interested in the table index and the interface name.

```
$ snmptable -Cbi db1 ifX | awk '{print $1,$2}' | column -t
...
index   Name
1       lo
2       enp0s3
3       enp0s8
```

Interface 1 is lo, interface 2 is enp0s3, and interface 3 is enp0s8. Let's see which IP addresses are attached to each interface by checking the IP address table ipAddrTable.

```
$ snmptable -Cb db1 ipAddrTable
SNMP table: RFC1213-MIB::ipAddrTable
```

Addr	IfIndex	NetMask	BcastAddr	ReasmMaxSize
127.0.0.1	1	255.0.0.0	0	?
203.0.113.206	2	255.255.255.0	1	?

---

22   A shocking number of organizations don't understand that when they buy new servers or other equipment, they must also allocate funding for the infrastructure and staff for that gear.

The `ifIndex` column refers to the interface number in the interface table. Interfaces 1 and 2 have an IP address. Interface 3, `enp0s8`, does not. That's a good hint that this host isn't really using interface 3, unless it's a member of some virtual interface like a bridge. Let's verify its activity by checking how much traffic this host is passing on that interface. Examining the headers of `ifXTable` reveals `HCInOctets` and `HCOutOctets` in columns 7 and 11 respectively. Those look promising. Searching this host's snmpbulkwalk output shows that the full OIDs are `IF-MIB::ifHCInOctets` and `IF-MIB::ifHCOutOctets`, and that they represent the number of bytes that have passed through this interface since the host booted. Let's view those values.

```
$ snmptable -Cbi dbl ifX | awk '{print $2,$7,$11}' | column -t
table:
Name     HCInOctets   HCOutOctets
lo       28904902     28904902
enp0s3   205287369    91156320
enp0s8   178829       5242
```

The interface `enp0s8` has done almost nothing. Any connected and up interface will receive and transmit Ethernet frames, but without an IP address we can be pretty sure there's nothing happening here. View this counter a few times to see if the number is incrementing, just to be sure.

Let's check the interface's administrative status.

```
$ snmpbulkwalk dbl ifAdminStatus
IF-MIB::ifAdminStatus.1 = INTEGER: up(1)
IF-MIB::ifAdminStatus.2 = INTEGER: up(1)
IF-MIB::ifAdminStatus.3 = INTEGER: up(1)
```

All three interfaces are up. Interface 3 is disused. Let's turn it off.

This object has a type of Integer, so we'll use the i flag. But what are the valid values, and what do they mean? Running `snmptranslate -Td IF-MIB::ifAdminStatus` tells us that 1 means "up," 2 means "down," and 3 means "testing." Let's make this interface administratively down with snmpset.

```
$ snmpset db1 IF-MIB::ifAdminStatus.3 i 2
IF-MIB::ifAdminStatus.3 = INTEGER: down(2)
```

Checking the `ifAdminStatus` OIDs shows that this interface is now down. If your network administrator is watching their switch, they'll see a port go offline.[23]

You could also use interface management for rebooting PoE devices, or having your IDS close interfaces that repeatedly match a virus signature.

READ-CREATE

Vendors have used SET for all sorts of operations. For objects that have a MAX-ACCESS of read-create, you can use complicated SET commands to add rows to tables. The SNMPv3 user management commands use this feature to manage users and views. Embedded devices might use this for routes, ARP entries, or whatever the vendor's twisted mind can conceive. You'll need to provide snmpset(1) several objects as arguments, in the correct order. As the exact syntax varies by agent, object, and vendor, and there are no broad use cases, I won't give examples. You should be aware this exists, though, and if you see a long snmpset(1) command you should consider if it's adding rows to a table.

As a last point, SET operations are atomic. Either the change completes successfully, or the whole SET is cancelled. This isn't so important when you're changing a single object, but if you're creating entire rows it's vital.

Armed with the OID and data type, you can change any writable object in the MIB. You are now equipped to truly foul up your hosts. If that's not enough, let's discuss running multiple SNMP agents simultaneously.

---

23   Experienced network administrators document what's plugged into each port. They know better than to trust that documentation, but they *have* it.

Chapter 8: Proxies, SMUX, and AgentX

No programmer or protocol designer can anticipate all possible real-world deployments of their tools, or predict what someone will need from their software in five or ten years. The best software is either so simple it won't require expansion, such as cat(1) and ed(1), or is deliberately extensible. SNMP agents can be extended through use of proxies, SMUX, and AgentX.

An agent acting as an SNMP *proxy* receives requests and forwards them to another agent. This is the oldest method of extending an agent, and it's still likely to work with all but the most recalcitrant software.

A single SNMP agent can't understand every single program that might run on a host. It's not uncommon for a program to include a small SNMP agent that understands only enough about SNMP to handle queries about the program's functions. A subagent for a routing daemon knows enough to provide routes, route sources, and protocol information in accordance with the daemon's MIB. A subagent for a database understands how many transactions are pending, how many rows have been updated, and so on. A *master agent* handles the network, authentication, and all that boring SNMP protocol stuff, but queries the subagent regarding a particular MIB. SNMP has two subagent protocols, SMUX and AgentX.

SMUX is the original subagent protocol. Released in 1991, it is officially deprecated and should not be used. Net-snmp still supports it. Some software hasn't caught on yet, however, so we'll briefly discuss both using and disabling it.

The modern standard for SNMP extensions is the *Agent Extensibility Protocol*, usually called *AgentX*. As a sysadmin, I find AgentX the most painless way to make agents interoperate. We'll use AgentX to query third-party software and to improve net-snmp performance.

Not all agents support all three methods. Not all software supports all of these interoperability methods. I've had good luck finding AgentX agents for the particular mix of software I most often use. Other sysadmins tell me that they can't find any AgentX agents, but have good luck with proxies, or SMUX. Still others tell me that proxies cause spontaneous human combustion in the accounting department, but I'm fairly certain that the accountants are trying to blame us innocent IT folks for the consequences of their dread rites. Learn the options. See which inflicts the least harm on you.

Proxies

Not all SNMP agents support the same features. You might discover that you want to use one agent for one feature, but another agent for a different feature. You can run two agents on the same host, but they can't listen on the same network port. Having a manager query two different ports for two different services causes confusion. Ideally, you'll run one agent as a subagent of the other. Not all agents support SMUX or AgentX, however. In this case, combine the agents by having one agent delegate, or *proxy*, certain MIBs for the other. A proxy agent accepts SNMP queries normally, but when queried for select MIB trees it makes its own query to another agent and returns that answer.

Why would you use a proxy? Some software—the Squid proxy, for example—includes an SNMP agent. These agents often run on an alternate port. I'd like to integrate those agents into the host's primary agent.

Sometimes an operating system includes an SNMP agent that supports OS-specific features not found in snmpd. FreeBSD's snmp agent, bsnmpd, provides FreeBSD-specific objects via an enterprise MIB, but it doesn't support a bunch of features in net-snmp's snmpd.

I'll use both of these as examples.

Configuring Secondary Agents

The agent to be proxied must be configured to listen on a different network port. Ideally, it listens on only the **localhost** address.

The secondary agent also needs access control, but it doesn't need to match that used by the primary agent. If the proxied agent is running on the same host, and will be queried over the loopback address, you can even use communities. If you're proxying an agent elsewhere on the network, you want authentication at least as strong as your master agent. Our examples all proxy on the local host and use communities.

Verify that the secondary agent works by querying it on its native ports. While you probably know of at least one MIB you want to make available via proxy, I encourage you to perform a complete snmpbulkwalk to check for other interesting MIBs.

bsnmpd(8)

Configure the FreeBSD native agent, bsnmpd(8), in /etc/snmpd.config.

I need the agent to listen on 127.0.0.1 on UDP port 1161. Use the *begemotSnmpdPortStatus* keyword. The keyword includes the address and port, as shown below.

```
begemotSnmpdPortStatus.127.0.0.1.1161 = 1
```

The *snmpd.config* keyword *read* sets the community, and defaults to **public**. Here I tell bsnmpd to accept the SNMPv2 read-only community **insecureRO**.

```
read := "insecureRO"
```

Enable any desired bsnmp modules such as PF, netgraph, and so on, then enable bsnmpd.

```
# sysrc bsnmpd_enable=YES
```

Once that's done, run a complete SNMP query on the local host. Do not try to set up proxy access until you know the proxy will reach something.

```
$ snmpbulkwalk -v2c -c insecureRO localhost:1161 .1
```

Studying the results shows that the only MIB bsnmpd offers that snmpd doesn't is .1.3.6.1.4.1.12325, the FreeBSD-specific BEGEMOT-SNMPD-MIB. Grab the MIB file from your FreeBSD host. We'll set up snmpd to proxy that OID.

Squid

Configure Squid's SNMP agent in *squid.conf*. The configuration has two parts: setting up the network and configuring the community. Grab the MIB file SQUID-MIB.txt from the Squid install and copy it to your agent. Use the *snmp_port* keyword to set the port it listens on and *snmp_incoming_address* to attach to an address. We'll use Squid's standard SNMP port of 3401 and bind the agent to **localhost**.

```
snmp_port 3401
snmp_incoming_address 127.0.0.1
```

Configure a community with Squid's access control lists. As this query won't traverse the network, we'll use SNMPv2c. We'll lock this down to access from **localhost** as well.

```
acl snmppublic snmp_community cacheInsecureRO
snmp_access allow snmppublic localhost
snmp_access deny all
```

Restart Squid, and you should have a working SNMP agent. Test it by running snmpbulkwalk on the Squid server.

```
$ snmpbulkwalk -v2c -c cacheInsecureRO \
    localhost:3401 enterprise
```

If it works, you're ready. Copy the Squid SNMP agent's authentication information for use in your SNMP proxy. If it doesn't work, check the Squid logs to see what it's complaining about.

Configuring Snmpd to Proxy

As the primary agent, net-snmp's snmpd should be set up to listen on port 161 and use your standard authentication methods.

Use the *snmpd.conf* keyword *proxy* to tell snmpd to query another agent. You must know the first OID of the MIB you want to forward, and valid snmpget(1) or snmpbulkwalk(1) arguments to make those queries.

```
proxy <command arguments> <first OID>
```

We already ran an snmpbulkwalk against our proxied bsn-mpd agent. Querying that agent required the arguments -v2c -c insecureRO localhost:1161. We've also identified the MIB that we want to forward: .1.3.6.1.4.1.12325. This gives us an *snmpd.conf* entry like this.

```
proxy -v2c -c insecureRO localhost:1161 .1.3.6.1.4.1.12325
```

We also have a Squid agent that we can interrogate with -v2c -c cacheInsecureRO localhost:3401. We want to forward the OID .1.3.6.1.4.1.3495, so our configuration is like this.

```
proxy -v2c -c cacheInsecureRO localhost:3401 .1.3.6.1.4.1.3495
```

Restart snmpd and bulkwalk the agent's enterprise MIB from your manager.

```
$ snmpbulkwalk squid3 enterprise
...
SQUID-MIB::cacheSysVMsize.0 = INTEGER: 216
SQUID-MIB::cacheSysStorage.0 = INTEGER: 0
SQUID-MIB::cacheUptime.0 = Timeticks: (121104) 0:20:11.04
...
BEGEMOT-SNMPD-MIB::begemotSnmpdTransmitBuffer.0 = INTEGER: 2048
BEGEMOT-SNMPD-MIB::begemotSnmpdReceiveBuffer.0 = INTEGER: 2048
BEGEMOT-SNMPD-MIB::begemotSnmpdCommunityDisable.0 = INTEGER: true(1)
...
```

As far as the manager is concerned, they've queried a single agent. The answer includes SQUID-MIB, the net-snmp-only enterprise MIBs, and flows seamlessly into the bsnmpd-only BEGEMOT-SNMPD-MIB.

While net-snmp's snmpd can proxy any number of agents, I would encourage you to only proxy agents on the local hosts.

It is possible to remap OIDs so that you can make a proxied agent's entire MIB available through the proxy, or to proxy multiple devices. Most often, these are solutions to problems better solved at the network level. If you have a notably uncooperative network, however, check the net-snmp documentation to see how to deploy these.

SMUX

SMUX is an early agent multiplexing protocol. The successor protocol, AgentX, escaped in 1998, and no new software should be written to use SMUX. If the stars fall into their most horrid alignment, however, you might be trapped into using SMUX. While snmpd cannot act as an SMUX subagent, it accepts connections from SMUX subagents. An SMUX subagent is technically called a *peer*, although it is in no way the main agent's equal.

SMUX Configuration

SMUX peers authenticate each other using a password and an OID. When the subagent starts, it contacts the primary agent and declares "I would like to serve this OID, and here is my password." If the master agent has a matching OID and password configured, it delegates responsibility for that OID to the subagent.

Configure snmpd to accept a SMUX connection with the *smuxpeer* keyword. It takes two arguments, the OID and the password.

```
smuxpeer oid password
```

Suppose your network still runs AppleTalk. It's rare these days, but so is SMUX. AppleTalk has its own MIB, .1.3.6.1.2.1.13. Here I tell `snmpd.conf` to delegate this MIB to an SMUX peer that identifies itself with the password *veryObsolete*.

```
smuxpeer .1.3.6.1.2.1.13 veryObsolete
```

Best of all, of course, is to eliminate the need for SMUX.

SMUX Networking

TCP port 199 is reserved for SMUX. Snmpd defaults to listening for SMUX on all IP addresses. Even if you're using SMUX, you're almost certainly using it on the local host. Change the IP address SMUX uses with the *smuxsocket* keyword. Here I tell snmpd to only listen on **localhost**.

```
smuxsocket 127.0.0.1
```

Ignoring the external network is your best choice for SMUX.

Disabling SMUX

Snmpd doesn't have a configuration file option to turn SMUX off, but you can disable the module. Use the `-I -smux` argument to snmpd. I usually disable SMUX just to keep junior sysadmins from asking me what's listening on port 199.

AgentX

The modern SNMP extension protocol is AgentX. AgentX is more flexible and stable than SMUX, and has been the standard for decades now. We'll look at configuring snmpd as an AgentX primary agent and using a MySQL subagent. In Chapter 10, we'll discuss using snmpd as both an agent and a subagent, to deal with possible problems with extensions.

AgentX Primary

Enable snmpd(8) as a primary agent with the *master agentx* keyword.

```
master agentx
```

This creates a Unix socket at */var/agentx/master*.

The primary agent can also set permissions on the socket. By default, the socket is owned by the user running **snmpd** and can only be accessed by that user. Most commonly, this is **root** and whatever group has GID 0 on your Unix. Depending on how your subagents are designed, you might need to set up a group that can access the socket. Use the *agentXPerms* keyword to set permissions.

```
agentXPerms socketpermissions directorypermissions user group
```

Later keywords can be dropped if not needed. All permissions must be in octal format (chmod(1)).

The minimal case, where you set the permissions on the directory, has very little practical use. You could set a subagent to run as part of the root group, but this is terrible security practice. This is anything but best practice, but if you're stuck you can do it. Here I grant group write permissions to the AgentX socket.

```
agentXPerms 660
```

The group also needs access to that directory for these permissions to work. This setting won't change the permissions on an existing directory; it only affects how the directory is created. Even if you change the directory's permissions manually, setting this is a good idea. You don't know what'll happen in the future.

```
agentXPerms 660 640
```

An agent needs access to change the underlying host, so it will almost always run as **root**. Running subagents as the **root** group is an abhorrent practice. Create a group for subagents, and assign subagent programs to that group. Here I provide an AgentX socket owned by the user **root** and the group **agentx**, and accessible to the group.

```
agentXPerms 660 640 root agentx
```

Add any program that provides AgentX to the group **agentx**, and they will be able to access the socket. Running multiple subagents is very common. Software like dnsdist provides an AgentX subagent, while many DNS servers require MariaDB or MySQL, so you'd use subagents for both.

While the defaults work for almost everyone, setting *agentXPerms* lets you work around a wide variety of unutterable software horrors.

MySQL Subagent

While many programs offer AgentX subagents, MySQL is one of the most commonly deployed databases in the world.[24] If you want to monitor MySQL activity via SNMP, check out mysql-snmp available at https://github.com/masterzen/mysql-snmp. It's a Perl daemon that reads MySQL or MariaDB information and acts as an SNMP subagent. If you want to track how your database behaves by SNMP, this is how you do it.

---

24   If you must use MySQL, try MariaDB instead. It's MySQL, but untainted by Oracle. Other commercial MySQL variants also exist, if you need a support contract that doesn't involve phrases like "immortal soul" or "first-born child."

The mysql-snmp program requires a database login. Don't use **root** or another administrative account: rather, create an account just for monitoring. Once you have this account and verify that it works, we can configure mysql-snmp.

It is possible to set most mysql-snmp options on the command line, but don't do it. Command line options are visible to other users, and processes owned by unprivileged users. You don't want other users to see mysql-snmp's MySQL account information. While mysql-snmp reads options in standard *my.cnf* format, don't use the system's default *my.cnf*. You don't want to hard-code your account information in that file for all MySQL programs to read, either. Create a configuration file *mysql-snmp.cnf* to provide any needed username, password, and connection information.

```
[client]
user=monitor
password=PutRealPasswordHere
```

Use the −c command-line option to point mysql-snmp at the configuration file. You'll want to set this in the startup script.

```
# mysql-snmp -c /etc/mysql-snmp.cnf
```

Mysql-snmp automatically registers itself as an AgentX subagent at startup.

Now grab the MYSQL-SERVER-MIB.txt file included with the program. Copy it to your *$HOME/.snmp/mibs* directory. Run an snmpbulkwalk. The MySQL MIB is under .1.3.6.1.4.1.20267.

```
$ snmpbulkwalk database1 .1.3.6.1.4.1.20267
MYSQL-SERVER-MIB::myKeyReadRequests.0 = Counter32: 918
MYSQL-SERVER-MIB::myKeyReads.0 = Counter32: 1619
...
```

You can now track, graph, and visualize all sorts of MySQL information, giving you all the administrative support necessary to get the boss to order that really big server.

Agent-Subagent Communication

Not all the world is net-snmp, and not all SNMP agents communicate exactly like snmpd. You'll probably need to change how snmpd behaves to communicate with other agents.

Not all agents listen on the Unix socket `/var/agentx/master`. The *agentXSocket* keyword lets you define different locations, or even network addresses, for both master agent and subagent. Some agents only work with TCP/IP. Other agents can't be granted permissions to `/var/agentx/master` without horribly violating system integrity. TCP port 705 is reserved for AgentX.

```
agentXSocket tcp:localhost:705
```

You can also adjust timing and retries for AgentX requests. The master agent defaults to giving the subagents one second to respond to each request, and retrying each request five times. You might need to increase those limits. The *agentXTimeout* keyword sets how long the master agent gives a subagent to respond. It takes a number of seconds as an argument. The *agentXRetries* keyword sets a number of times the master agent will retry the request. If you change these, set them on both the subagent and the master agent.

The SNMP manager will probably time out its request in five seconds, so don't increase timeouts too greatly unless the manager also uses increased limits.

Subagents that lose contact with their master agents try to reconnect every 15 seconds. If you must change this interval, use the *agentXPingInterval* keyword and the desired number of seconds.

Now that you can set up subagents, let's look at access control.

Chapter 9: Access Control

We've seen how to restrict access to an SNMP agent by SNMPv3 username or, for older protocol versions, communities. But once someone has valid credentials, they get unlimited agent access. Yes, you can set usernames and communities to read-only access, but there's lots of reasons you might want people to view only part of a host's MIB.

Achieve all this and more with SNMP's View-Based Access Control Model, *VACM*. While we'll use net-snmp to learn VACM, anything that supports SNMPv3 should support VACM. We'll also touch on the slightly simpler access control configuration net-snmp supports, but successfully deploying it requires a certain understanding of the concepts behind VACM.

Credentials are separate from access control. You'll create users with snmpusm, but that is an entirely separate process from granting them access to the MIB.

Designing Access

A small environment is probably more cooperative and open than a big one: either you have SNMP authentication information, or you don't. Therefore we'll configure VACM to comply with the standards of a huge global corporation with divisions, sub-divisions, and different teams that have differing degrees of cooperation and competition. Some of these divisions were once independent companies acquired by the organization, and are not wholly trusted by the old hands. In a big organization where people argue about every infuriating irrelevant detail, restricting different groups to different parts of the MIB is often the simplest way to prevent arguments.

Gather information for every manager that needs access. What username, usernames, or communities do they use? What security level is appropriate? Does their traffic originate from a restricted range of IP addresses? What objects do they need read-only access to, and which do they need read-write access for? Save yourself later trouble and record these OIDs before starting. You can use the OID in any form recognized by interactive SNMP commands. I'm biased towards numerical OIDs, but you can choose your own path to madness. Review your snmpbulk-walk output and use snmptranslate to figure out the proper OIDs.

Put this information in a table or spreadsheet. Not only will that ensure you have everything you need, executive types often believe that spreadsheet generation validates employees' continued existence.

Sample Environment

Here's a policy from a real company, thinly disguised as DagonCorp.

Systems on the private network sometimes go bonkers and send traffic to places they shouldn't. A network administrator confronted with strange traffic would need to poke at the source IP to see what's going on. Everyone in the company can therefore use the community name **dagon** to interrogate the system group, .1.3.6.1.2.1.1, in SNMPv2-MIB, via either SNMPv1 or SNMPv2c. This group contains the hostname, system description, responsible person, and related minutia.[25] The company uses the IP addresses 203.0.113.0/24, 192.0.2.0/24, and 2001:db8::/32 internally; all **dagon** queries must come from those addresses.

The network management system gets read access with the username **monitor**. As monitoring increases network traffic and system load, and our monitoring team is overenthusiastic, we allow this user access to only the MIBs .1.3.6.1.4.1.2021.11 and .1.3.6.1.4.1.2021.2. Monitoring is not confidential, so the manager must authenticate but doesn't need privacy. A real network management system would need access to many more OIDs, but we'll make an example of these two.

---

25   While you would certainly push for such queries to use SNMPv3, not all IT departments everywhere in the world have sufficiently competent staff. Take what you can get from backwaters like Silicon Valley.

The host is a database server. The organization allows both MySQL variants and PostgreSQL. MySQL's subagent MIB is under `.1.3.6.1.4.1.20267`, while PostgreSQL's MIB is at `.1.3.6.1.4.1.27645`. The database team's monitoring system needs read-write access to these MIBs, and read access to the rest of the MIB. Thanks to past abuses, they are forbidden to read any of the SNMPv3 user information under `.1.3.6.1.6` and `.1.3.6.1.4.1.8072`. Their monitoring system's username is **dba**, and they need both authentication and privacy. (If individuals needed SNMP access, I would give each their own username and add them to a **dba** group.)

The system administration team responsible for this host get unfettered read-write access to the entirety of the MIB tree via the username **sysadmin**. They also need authentication and privacy.

User Validation

More than once, I've fought with SNMP access control configuration only to discover that I had incorrect authentication information for the underlying accounts. Create all users and communities before starting, and verify that all authentication is correct with an *snmpd.conf* snippet like this.

```
rouser    monitor    auth
rouser    dba        priv
rouser    sysadmin   priv
rocommunity  dagon
```

Once all users can do an snmpget or snmpbulkwalk, and you verify they aren't blocked by packet filters or proxies or some other interloper, remove these users from *snmpd.conf*. We'll first configure all access via VACM so that you can understand SNMP access control.

When the time comes for the end-user to validate their account, remind them that a walk starting at the `system` group might not show everything they're permitted access to. They'll get the best results by starting their walk at .1.

```
$ snmpbulkwalk www1 .1
```

These requirements look fairly complicated, but they'll work well for learning VACM. We'll also use the simplified configuration to meet as many of these requirements as we can.

Configuring VACM

VACM has five parts: context, security level names, groups, views, and access.

The *context* is the SNMP context, which we've mostly ignored. It's a mandated part of VACM, but not widely useful. Most often it's empty, as shown by empty double quotes (""). We will use context briefly in Chapter 12.

A *security name* is an SNMPv3 user. You can use SNMPv1 and SNMPv2c communities in VACM by mapping the communities to a security name.

A *group* is a collection of security names. It's the SNMP equivalent of */etc/group*.

A *view* creates a single coherent subset of a MIB. It's mostly used for access control.

An *access* rule says "This group can access this view." Access statements are where read and write privileges are assigned.

Despite the fancy names, VACM is a completely standard access control list. You create users and groups. You create lists of stuff people can and cannot access. You assign each group to a list. That's it. VACM imposes certain best practices—access is only given to groups, not to individual users.

Here's how we connect these components together to build our sample policy.

Security Names

SNMPv3 users are already recognized as VACM security names. We must convert our community name **dagon** to a VACM security name via *com2sec* and *com2sec6* statements. Use *com2sec* for IPv4 traffic, and *com2sec6* for IPv6. Each statement takes three arguments: the new security name, the manager's IP address, and the community name.

Here I create the security name **corporate**, using the company's internal IP addresses and the community name **dagon**.

```
com2sec corporate 203.0.113.0/24 dagon
com2sec corporate 192.0.2.0/24 dagon
com2sec6 corporate 2001:db8::/32 dagon
```

This gives me a total of four security names: **monitor**, **dba**, **sysadmin**, and **corporate**.

Groups

Attach users to groups with a *group* statement. Even if a group has only one user, you still must create a group for that user. Only groups can be selectively granted access to the MIB via VACM. A *group* statement requires a group name, the security model for that entry, and a security name. You've seen all of these except for the security model.

The group security model describes the network security this group uses. The most common entries are *usm* (SNMPv3 users), *v1* (SNMPv1 communities), and *v2c* (SNMPv2c communities). Each unique combination of group name, security model, and security name requires its own *group* statement, adding this combination of security name and security model to the group. I'm naming my group after the primary user, adding **_group** to the end.

Take a look at how we create a group for our company-wide old-style community **dagon**, as mapped into the security name **corporate**.

```
group corporate_group v1  corporate
group corporate_group v2c corporate
group corporate_group usm monitor
group corporate_group usm dba
group corporate_group usm sysadmin
```

The community name **dagon** doesn't appear anywhere here. Groups don't accept community names; that's why the *com2sec* and *com2sec6* keywords exist. Each entry starts with the *group* keyword, to show we're creating a group. Then comes the group name. I named this group **corporate_group**. Then we have the security type. SNMPv1 and SNMPv2c each require their own entry. Finally, we have the security name created for the company-wide community.

With these two lines, all permitted SNMPv1 and SNMPv2c queries are lumped into the group **corporate_group**. We can treat them as a single entity.

The various departments will also want access to the public information. While this wasn't specified in the design document we got from the Powers That Be, we know perfectly well users are going to complain about not having access to the system group. We want to get ahead of the sniveling, so we add them to **corporate_group**, using the *usm* security model.

Also create groups for the SNMPv3 users, all with the *usm* security model.

```
group monitor_group    usm monitor
group dba_group         usm dba
group sysadmin_group   usm sysadmin
```

Each user must have its own line. When the database team suffers its inevitable MySQL-PostgreSQL internecine iconoclasm, we'll probably have to create separate users for them. Seeing as hosts without PostgreSQL won't return PostgreSQL objects, and hosts without MySQL won't respond to MySQL objects, we could put them in the same group.

```
group dba_group usm mysql
group dba_group usm postgresql
```

With groups set up, you can now turn your attention to views.

Views

A *view* is a list of OIDs. A view might be "the `system` MIB group," "everything in the MIB except these certain OIDs and their children," or any combination of objects. Views are used for access control, but are not access control statements in themselves. Configure views with a *view* statement. A *view* statement has four components: the keyword *view*, the view name, the word *included* or *excluded*, and an OID.

I'm naming each view after the users that the view is built for, adding *_view* at the end.

The *included* and *excluded* keywords allow and deny access to different OIDs. A view that uses only *included* keywords assumes that the view includes only the objects stated. A view that uses only *excluded* keywords assumes that anything not explicitly excluded is included. A view that combines both includes part of the MIB, but excludes the specified subsections.

Consider the company-wide view that allows access to the `system` MIB group.

```
view corporate_view included system
```

The *view* keyword declares this to be a view. The view name is *corporate_view*. We are explicitly including OIDs, specifically those in the *system* MIB group, so the rest of the MIB is not included in the view.

A view that includes multiple separate object trees needs multiple lines. Here we set the view *monitor_view* to include two separate parts of the MIB. This is a very small, narrow view.

```
view monitor_view included .1.3.6.1.4.1.2021.11
view monitor_view included .1.3.6.1.4.1.2021.2
```

The view *dba-rw_view* is very similar to *monitor_view*. It includes different objects, because this view is for a different group of people.

```
view dba-rw_view included .1.3.6.1.4.1.20267
view dba-rw_view included .1.3.6.1.4.1.27645
```

Here's a view that doesn't include select parts of the tree.

```
view dba-ro_view excluded .1.3.6.1.6
view dba-ro_view excluded .1.3.6.1.4.1.8072
```

Finally, we have a view that includes absolutely everything.

```
view sysadmin_view included .1
```

A view can also include a mask, used to include only a single line of a table. This was originally intended to allow customers access to all of the objects for their interface, and folks had other ideas on how it could be deployed. It was rarely used when it was created, those additional uses never materialized, and it almost never appears today because allowing customers read access to provider equipment is a terrible idea. For every user that thoughtfully uses such access, another queries their provider's gear thirty times a second. If customers need interface information, give them an account on your monitoring system that lets them view their statistics. Everyone will be happier.[26]

We are now equipped to assign privileges to users.

Access

An *access* statement assigns permissions to a combination of a single view and a single group. This is where you say this group can read but not write a view, or both read and write. (You could also allow a group write-only access, not permitting it to read what it can write to. I would call this completely daft, except that I'm certain someone—or some *thing*—had a horrifying but legitimate use case for it.) It also lets you set security privileges. In case of conflicts, the last matching rule wins.

An access statement has nine fields, but some of them are not generally used.

```
access group context secmodel seclevel contextmatch \
    readview writeview trap
```

---

26   Except that customer who wants to query your router thirty times a second, and he doesn't deserve happiness.

The first field always is the keyword *access*.

The second field is the group name.

The third field is the SNMP context. For almost all agents, this will be an empty pair of double quotes ("").

The fourth field is the security model. You could use this to make rules that apply only to SNMPv3 users, or communities, or SNMP over TLS, and so on. We set security models in our groups, and declaring one here increases the odds of misconfiguration. Set this to *any*.

The fifth field is SNMPv3 security level. Set it to *noauth*, *auth*, or *priv*, as you want to demand from the user. Access for community-based groups always use *noauth*, as communities have no authentication or privacy mechanism.

The sixth field is for matching contexts. For normal use, set this to *exact* to declare the command must exactly match the context name.

The seventh field configures read access. Put the name of a view here.

The eighth field configures write access. If the group has write access to a view, put the view name here. Otherwise, put *none*.

Lastly, we have a field to list a view for TRAP and INFORM requests. Almost nobody uses this. Put *none* here.

Consider this entry for our fellow corporate employees around the world.

```
access corporate_group  "" any noauth exact corporate_view none none
```

We're allowing **corporate_group** access to this agent. The third and fourth fields are always "" any, as discussed above. As **corporate_group** uses communities, the fifth field must be *noauth*. The sixth field is set to *exact* in all access rules. Next we assign a view with read access: that's *corporate_view*. The eighth field is for views with read-write access. We can't trust our corporate peers to send an email when they see a problem, so there's no way they're getting write access to our hosts. Set this to *none*. Finally, the ninth field is always *none*.

Here are the rest of our access rules.

```
access monitor_group  "" any auth exact monitor_view  none        none
access dba_group       "" any priv exact dba-ro_view   none        none
access dba_group       "" any priv exact dba-rw_view   dba-rw_view none
access sysadmin_group  "" any priv exact sysadmin_view sysadmin_view none
```

Group **monitor_group**, for monitoring, needs authentication but not privacy, so their security level is set to *auth*. The "read" column gives them access to the view *monitor_view*, but the "write" column is set to *none*. They have read-only access to this view.

The group **dba_group** is more complicated. They need authentication and privacy on all queries, so the security level is set to *priv*. The first **dba_group** line grants read-only access to the view *dba-ro_view*, much like the rule for **monitor_group**. The second **dba_group** line grants both read and write access to the view *dba-rw_view*.

Our last access statement, for the group **sysadmin_group**, requires authentication and privacy. It has both read and write access to the view *sysadmin_view*.

Follow this model any time you need a complete VACM setup. Net-snmp's configuration mimics the standards. Vendors who write their own SNMP agents probably have their own improved, incomprehensible syntax, but if they support VACM the basic ideas of security names, groups, views, and access controls should be in there somewhere.[27]

If a vendor expects you to configure all VACM-based access control via SNMP, or if you must script access control across a large network, take a look at snmpvacm(1).

---

27   Learning proprietary gibberish is *so* much easier when you're not simultaneously learning the technology's underlying concepts.

VACM Expansion

These examples are deliberately short and simple. In reality, I'd expect a single view to include dozens of *included* statements, and probably a couple *excluded* statements to hide certain MIB subtrees. Like any access control system, your VACM configuration will expand beyond all reasonable limits.

The best advice I can offer is to start with limited access, and only expand it when people complain.

Now that you understand how this fits together, let's see how snmpd simplifies it.

Simplified snmpd Access Control

While net-snmp has a fairly complete VACM configuration, most of us don't need anything near that. Most of us don't need contexts, or specialized security levels outside of those set in the group definition. For many of us, group definitions are overkill and our MIB restrictions are a very simple "allow this MIB."

Net-snmp supports a simplified access control configuration with the *rouser* and *rwuser* keywords. You can also use the *rocommunity* and *rwcommunity* keywords for older SNMP versions. Using these properly requires understanding views and security levels, however, so be sure to read the previous section.

Our examples here build on the sample environment discussed at the beginning of this chapter. For complex MIB restrictions, you must understand views as the preceding VACM section discussed.

SNMPv3 User Access

Each user can be assigned only one of *rwuser* or *rouser*. A *rwuser* or *rouser* keyword has the following format.

```
rXuser <username> <securitylevel> <OID or -V and view>
```

The username is an SNMPv3 user.

For security, use one of *noauth*, *auth*, or *priv*. If you don't specify a security level, it defaults to *auth*.

An OID can be given numerically, or by any text recognized by an SNMP manager command. For more complicated lists that need a view, use *-V* and the view name.

You can skip the OID or view if you don't need to restrict it. If you don't need to restrict the OID and *auth* security is sufficient, drop both terms.

Simplified views are very similar to VACM views. The major difference is that they default to not permitting access. If you want to exclude specific OIDs from a simplified view, you must explicitly allow the rest of the MIB.

Our user **sysadmin** needs read-write access to the entire MIB, with privacy. No view or OID is needed.

```
rwuser sysadmin priv
```

The user **monitor** only needs authentication, no privacy. It needs read-only access to more than one OID, so use *-V* to assign it access to the view *monitor_view*.

```
view monitor_view included .1.3.6.1.4.1.2021.2
view monitor_view included .1.3.6.1.4.1.2021.11
rouser monitor auth -V monitor_view
```

Using simplified configuration for the database team's access won't work. Each user can be assigned either read-only access or read-write access. If you must have a single SNMPv3 user with mixed read-only and read-write access, you must use VACM. The only way around this with simplified configuration is create a **dbaro** and a **dbarw** user, and assign each separate access. It makes initial configuration easier, but vastly increases the number of complaint calls you get from the database team.

Our **dbaro** user is forbidden access to specific parts of the MIB, so we need a view. Remember, simplified access views that exclude OIDs must explicitly state that access to the rest of the MIB is permitted with an *included* statement, like so.

```
view dbaro_view excluded .1.3.6.1.6
view dbaro_view excluded .1.3.6.1.4.1.8072
view dbaro_view included .1
rwuser dbaro priv -V dbaro_view
```

The database team's read-write access user, **dbarw**, is permitted access to only certain OIDs.

```
view dbarwview included .1.3.6.1.4.1.20267
view dbarwview included .1.3.6.1.4.1.27645
rwuser dbarw priv -V dbarwview
```

This access emulates what we created with full-on VACM, except the database team has two usernames. They will complain. Use VACM instead.

Community Access

Community names, for SNMPv1 and SNMPv2c, can also use access control. While access controls permit intruders to spoof traffic, they help limit the scope of that damage. The simplified community access restrictions poorly emulate VACM, and is only suitable for basic rules.

Use the *rocommunity* and the *rwcommunity* keywords to configure IPv4 communities, and *rocommunity6* and *rwcommunity6* for IPv6 communities. The keywords use the following format.

```
rXcommunity <community name> <source address> <OID or -V view>
```

If a community doesn't have restricted access to the MIB, you can drop the OID or view term. If the community has neither IP address restrictions nor MIB restrictions, drop both.

Any one community name can have one and only one entry, either *rwcommunity* or *rocommunity*. You can't give a community one set of read-only permissions and a different set of read-write permissions. You can't give one community access from multiple IP address ranges. You can use the same community for IPv4 and IPv6, so long as there's only one entry for each IP protocol. The lack of multiple IP address restrictions makes simplified communities less flexible than simplified SNMPv3.

Our sample environment says that the community **dagon** gets read-only access to the `system` group from our internal IP addresses. Our organization has two ranges of internal IPv4 addresses, so we can't use simplified configuration for community names. Here's how we'd set this up if there was only one range of IPv4 addresses.

```
rocommunity dagon 203.0.113.0/24 system
rocommunity6 dagon 2001:db8::/32 system
```

If we need a view rather than a single MIB or OID, we can specify it with -*V*.

```
rocommunity dagon 203.0.113.0/24 -V dagoncorpview
```

Simple community-based configuration works for many organizations. Unless you're one of the disposable wretches employed by DagonCorp, of course.

So far in this book, we've twisted our minds to encompass SNMP. Let's get a little payback, and stretch SNMP to fit our most bizarre—well, okay, second-most, maybe third-most-bizarre—desires.

Chapter 10: Extending snmpd(8)

No matter how standard your environment is, at some point you'll have a problem that neither your application's developers nor the net-snmp developers considered. You'll need to extract previously unknown information from your host and make it available via SNMP. This requires extending the SNMP agent.

Net-snmp's snmpd has several extension features. If you're a programmer, chances are your favorite language has canned modules to get information into SNMP. Perl and Python are popular choices, but there are libraries for everything from Pascal to PowerBuilder.[28] You can execute shell commands directly within `snmpd.conf`.

We'll look at the two easiest methods to extend snmpd, the *extend* and *pass* keywords. Before that, let's discuss *where* to extend the MIB.

Custom Objects

While net-snmp provides objects for simple extensions, if you're doing something complicated you probably want to define your own object structure. The MIB is centrally managed, however. The ITU manages `.1`, and has delegated branches below that to other organizations. Don't grab a random OID: doing so karmically ensures that next year you'll have to install software that officially uses that OID. You can either use an experimental MIB, or apply for your own MIB.

The experimental MIB is `.1.3.6.1.3`. This MIB is specifically for organizations to play around in. It's rather like an RFC 6761 domain (example.org, 10.0.0.0/8, 172.16.0.0/12, 192.168.0.0/16, and so on): you can do anything you want with it, so long as you keep it private and it never leaves your organization or your business partners.

---

28   You can even find SNMP libraries for languages not beginning with "P."

Net-snmp also offers an experimental MIB in its enterprise MIB, `.1.3.6.1.4.1.8072.9999`. It's mainly intended for experimenting with net-snmp, but if you're not an SNMP developer you might as well use it.

You can get your own MIB, either from the Internet Authority for Assigned Numbers (IANA) or directly from the ITU. IANA controls the enterprise MIB, `.1.3.6.1.4`, and has delegated tens of thousands of OIDs to private organizations. If you intend to write code that will leave your organization, apply for your own delegation. People have received enterprise MIB delegations for far more trivial purposes than whatever you're doing. If you don't want to go to IANA, you can apply to ITU or national registries.

An organization typically only gets a single enterprise MIB. When you get your number, delegate each project an OID within that MIB. Once you start developing SNMP extensions for your software, you'll be surprised at how useful they can be.

But let's start by piggy-backing on net-snmp's auto-configuring OIDs.

Self-Configuring Extensions

The *extend* keyword empowers you to run shell commands from `snmpd.conf` without worrying too much about formatting the results or choosing OIDs. The results appear in a MIB that is written to accommodate almost any sort of data. The down side is, that data is not as highly formatted and normal as other MIBs. It's absurdly easy to implement, however, and if you keep the output of your commands brief it can be just as useful as anything in `ifXTable`.

Anyone who has access to your agent can read exactly what commands the extension runs. Write them so they can't be easily abused. Extending SNMP to run something like `sudo /bin/sh /tmp/command` is a great way to destroy system integrity.

The *extend* keyword takes at least two arguments, a name and a command. The command can include arguments.

Echo Extensions

As with all things Unix, we'll start by playing with echo(1). Here's an `snmpd.conf` configuration for an extension named "shoggoth" that spits out quoted text.

```
extend shoggoth /bin/echo "run away!"
```

Run the extensions and get the results by querying either of two tables, `nsExtendOutput1` and `nsExtendOutput2`, both in the MIB `NET-SNMP-EXTEND-MIB`. While normally you'd view tables with snmptable(1), a walk is more comprehensible for our single-entry table.

```
$ snmpbulkwalk www1 nsExtendOutput1
NET-SNMP-EXTEND-MIB::nsExtendOutput1Line."shoggoth" =
       STRING: run away!
NET-SNMP-EXTEND-MIB::nsExtendOutputFull."shoggoth" =
       STRING: run away!
NET-SNMP-EXTEND-MIB::nsExtendOutNumLines."shoggoth" =
       INTEGER: 1
NET-SNMP-EXTEND-MIB::nsExtendResult."shoggoth" =
       INTEGER: 0
```

We get four OIDs. Each OID ends with the name we assigned to our extension, in quotes. Once we have multiple extensions, we'll use this to pick out a particular one.

The first line, `nsExtendOutput1Line`, shows the first line of the command output.

The second line, `nsExtendOutputFull`, gives the complete output of the command. This extension has only one line of output, so it's identical to the previous entry.

The third line, `nsExtendOutNumLines`, gives the number of lines of output.

Finally, `nsExtendResult` gives the return code of the command. If a command returns anything other than 0, you have trouble.

The second table, `nsExtendOutput2`, presents each line of output as its own OID. This example isn't terribly exciting.

```
$ snmpbulkwalk www1 nsExtendOutput2
NET-SNMP-EXTEND-MIB::nsExtendOutLine."shoggoth".1 =
    STRING: run away!
```

The OID `NET-SNMP-EXTEND-MIB::nsExtendOut-`
`Line."shoggoth"` contains child OIDs for each line of the output.
Entry `.1` is the first line of output, `.2` would be the second, and so on.

Command Extensions

Let's try running a real command with *extend*. Comment out the
"shoggoth" line and try something like this.

```
extend files /bin/ls /tmp/files/
```

Whenever you run snmpbulkwalk against the extension OID, snmpd runs `ls /tmp/files`. Let's see how this changes things.

```
$ snmpbulkwalk www1 nsExtendOutput1
NET-SNMP-EXTEND-MIB::nsExtendOutput1Line."files" = STRING: customer1
NET-SNMP-EXTEND-MIB::nsExtendOutputFull."files" = STRING: customer1
problem8
systemd.core
NET-SNMP-EXTEND-MIB::nsExtendOutNumLines."files" = INTEGER: 3
NET-SNMP-EXTEND-MIB::nsExtendResult."files" = INTEGER: 0
```

Under `nsExtendOutput1Line`, we get the first line from the
command: "customer1."

The OID `nsExtendOutputFull` gives us the complete output.
It's broken up on multiple lines, because the command produces multiple lines of output. Most MIBs do not allow an OID to have a value
containing multiple lines, but the extension MIB is written very flexi-
bly. We see the files *customer1*, *problem8*, and *systemd.core*.

At the OID `nsExtendOutNumLines`, we see there are 3 lines of
output.

Finally, `nsExtendResult` shows that `ls /tmp/files` returned
0. It ran correctly.

The second extension table, `nsExtendOutput2`, looks very different than our echo example.

```
$ snmpbulkwalk www1 nsExtendOutput2
NET-SNMP-EXTEND-MIB::nsExtendOutLine."files".1 =
      STRING: customer1
NET-SNMP-EXTEND-MIB::nsExtendOutLine."files".2 =
      STRING: problem8
NET-SNMP-EXTEND-MIB::nsExtendOutLine."files".3 =
      STRING: systemd.core
```

We see nothing about the process behind the query. Instead, each line of output is a separate OID, allowing you to query each individually. An snmpbulkget(1) would let you retrieve an array of filenames.

Finding Specific OIDs

You don't want to pull a whole table into your management system and parse it to extract information. Escape quote marks in the `ex-tend` MIB with backslashes to use them on the command line. Use output modifiers like `-Ov` and `-OQ` (Chapter 3) to eradicate explanatory text.

```
$ snmpget -OvQ server1 \
      NET-SNMP-EXTEND-MIB::nsExtendOutputFull.\"files\"
customer1
problem8
systemd.core
```

If your management system chokes on escaped quotes, use snmptranslate to produce a completely numerical OID. Use whatever method works with your tools.

```
$ snmptranslate -Td -On \
      NET-SNMP-EXTEND-MIB::nsExtendOutputFull.\"files\"
.1.3.6.1.4.1.8072.1.3.2.3.1.2.5.102.105.108.101.115
nsExtendOutputFull OBJECT-TYPE
...
```

Note that the last five numbers in the resulting OID are the ASCII values for f, i, l, e, and s.

Maybe you don't care about the contents of the command output, but how much there is. Perhaps having more than 100 files in this directory is an error condition. That would make more than 100 lines of output. Grab the related `nsExtendOutNumLines` OID and stick it in your monitoring system. Again, use `-OvQ` to get rid of the explanatory text and just get a number.

```
$ snmpget -OvQ server1 \
    NET-SNMP-EXTEND-MIB::nsExtendOutNumLines.\"files\"
105
```

Set an alert level in your network management system, and you're good to go.

Extending to Shell Scripts

The *extend* keyword doesn't provide a shell, so useful shell constructs like && and | don't work. If you need those, you must write a shell script. Before writing the script, consider what you're going to do with the result. The output of snmpbulkwalk is already sufficiently horrid; you don't need to make it worse.[29]

Most often, we want our extension to return an integer that we can feed to our network management system. The NMS alarms when that integer passes a threshold. Keep the output from your script very simple: preferably, just a single number.

This script lets us remove our file count command from *snmpd.conf*.

```
#!/bin/sh

echo `/bin/ls /tmp/files | /usr/bin/wc -l`
```

Call it in *snmpd.conf* like so.

```
extend files /scripts/filecount.sh
```

Using external scripts rather than embedded extensions has advantages. Scripts are more easily expanded. You can change the script without restarting snmpd. On the downside, you can break the script without restarting snmpd. The extension doesn't care, it'll happily declare to your manager that the command won't run.

---

29   Unless you can make it worse with unique flair, in which case: go for it!

Caching and Timing

A deranged manager could query your agent many times a second. Your extension scripts impose load on the system, and while I'm sure you'll write them to be as light as possible, you don't want to run them dozens or hundreds of times in succession. Fortunately, when snmpd runs an extension it caches the command's output for five seconds. You can alter this timing, as well as a few other extension internals. This detail is all in the OID group nsExtendObjects, along with other extension information.

```
$ snmpbulkwalk server1 nsExtendObjects
NET-SNMP-EXTEND-MIB::nsExtendNumEntries.0 =
        INTEGER: 1
NET-SNMP-EXTEND-MIB::nsExtendCommand."files" =
        STRING: /bin/sh
NET-SNMP-EXTEND-MIB::nsExtendArgs."files" =
        STRING: /scripts/filecount.sh
NET-SNMP-EXTEND-MIB::nsExtendInput."files" =
        STRING:
NET-SNMP-EXTEND-MIB::nsExtendCacheTime."files" =
        INTEGER: 5
…
```

The nsExtendNumEntries.0 OID shows how many extend entries snmpd has in this MIB. We've only configured one, named "files."

The nsExtendCommand and nsExtendArgs OIDs give the command being run and its arguments. If you write your extensions foolishly, thinking that nobody will ever know you've left a big back door in the system: they can find out by asking.

The nsExtendInput OID reports the standard input for the command.

The nsExtendCacheTime OID shows how many seconds the results are cached. Change the cache time with an snmpset.

```
$ snmpset server1 \
  NET-SNMP-EXTEND-MIB::nsExtendCacheTime.\"files\" i 10
NET-SNMP-EXTEND-MIB::nsExtendCacheTime."files" =
     INTEGER: 10
```

This change is not written to the persistent data file.

In net-snmp 5.8 and newer, set a different cache time with the *-cacheTime* argument in `snmpd.conf`.

```
extend -cacheTime 90 files /bin/sh /scripts/filecount.sh
```

In older versions, permanently changing the cache time means adding an snmpset call to the `snmpd` startup script.

Multiple Extensions

What if you enable both of our sample extensions? The output gets intermingled just like any other table.

```
$ snmpbulkwalk www1 nsExtendOutput1
NET-SNMP-EXTEND-MIB::nsExtendOutput1Line."files" =
     STRING: customer1
NET-SNMP-EXTEND-MIB::nsExtendOutput1Line."shoggoth" =
     STRING: run away!
NET-SNMP-EXTEND-MIB::nsExtendOutputFull."files" =
     STRING: customer1
     problem8
     systemd.core
NET-SNMP-EXTEND-MIB::nsExtendOutputFull."shoggoth" =
     STRING: run away!
...
```

You can also view the results with snmptable, but disparate commands in a single table are not likely to be useful unless you're auditing your extensions.

Attaching Extensions to an OID

If you're not happy with letting snmpd auto-assign an OID to your extension, you can hard-code an OID in `snmpd.conf`. Put the desired root OID between the extend keyword and the name. Here I place my command at `.1` under the experimental OID `.1.3.6.1.3`.

```
extend .1.3.6.1.3.1 files /bin/sh /scripts/filecount.sh
```

You lose all name information when you run snmpbulkwalk or snmpget, however, and deciphering the output can be challenging. It's exactly the same as the result of walking nsExtendObjects, but numerical.

```
$ snmpbulkwalk server1 .1.3.6.1.3.1
SNMPv2-SMI::experimental.1.1.0 = INTEGER: 1
SNMPv2-SMI::experimental.1.2.1.2.7.47.98.105.110.47.115.104 =
     STRING: "/scripts/filecount.sh"
SNMPv2-SMI::experimental.1.2.1.3.7.47.98.105.110.47.115.104 = ""
SNMPv2-SMI::experimental.1.2.1.4.7.47.98.105.110.47.115.104 = ""
SNMPv2-SMI::experimental.1.2.1.5.7.47.98.105.110.47.115.104 =
     INTEGER: 5
SNMPv2-SMI::experimental.1.2.1.6.7.47.98.105.110.47.115.104 =
     INTEGER: 1
SNMPv2-SMI::experimental.1.2.1.7.7.47.98.105.110.47.115.104 =
     INTEGER: 1
...
SNMPv2-SMI::experimental.1.4.1.2.7.47.98.105.110.47.115.104.1 =
     STRING: "4"
```

If your script returns a single item, it's generally in the last OID returned. This is the equivalent of the table nsExtendOutput2 when it has a single entry. I see no advantage in using this long horrible OID versus the long and horrible but *labeled*[30] OID in the net-snmp extension MIB.

Customized Objects

The *extend* keyword lets you dump almost anything into SNMP, but its output is rather general. While the MIB is designed to be flexible enough to accommodate almost anything, sometimes you need a more specific structure. You must construct your MIB the way you need it. The *pass* keyword lets you pass an OID through to an external command, and lets that external command generate the responses as you decide. Your script must obey strict requirements for both input and output, no matter what kind of request the agent passes it.

---

30   Naming appalling entities doesn't make them less appalling, but it does give your brain a convenient bucket to contain the horror.

If you want to study a detailed example, the net-snmp wiki has links to examples of *pass* scripts in Bash and Perl and many people provide their scripts on source code sites. We'll generate a simple script for a couple basic extensions. You'll be running snmpd in debug mode for some of this, so be sure you're working on a test machine.

The agent blocks while running passthrough scripts. Make your passthrough scripts as efficient as possible. If you have trouble (but not before), consider moving the *pass* module into a subagent as discussed in Chapter 8.

We'll work at `.2` in the `experimental` MIB, or `.1.3.6.1.3.2`.

Before even starting, design your MIB.

MIB Design

You don't need to write a MIB file for your passthrough script. You must know what you want your script to do, and what sorts of values it should return, and how you'll structure your snmpbulkwalk output. My script will be `/script/pass.sh`.[31]

A basic script must handle GET and GETNEXT requests. While SET commands are certainly possible, safety demands careful input sanitization. I want the example script to be simple, so I won't demonstrate SET. Once you understand how the GET and GETNEXT requests work, anyone capable of performing that input sanitization properly won't have any trouble implementing changes via SET.

First, `pass.sh` will return the approximate number of entries in the packet filter state table as an integer. At one company I worked for, many years ago, the packet filter state table on one server filled up. The resulting outage meant that the company had to monitor the state table size on all servers until the end of time. (This monitoring is still in place, decades later.) This requires enabling a packet filter and configuring it to keep state.

---

31   I made extensive use of the example scripts while writing this, because I'm not *that* big of an idiot.

Second, `pass.sh` will return the first line of the file `/tmp/appstatus` as a string. The load balancer will check this object. If it's anything other than the string "OK" the host will be pulled from the load balancer pool. If you're testing this, you'll want to create that file. (If you use this type of configuration in real life, be sure you secure that file.)

I don't want to write a MIB file, but as my extensions grow I know I'll forget the exact interpretation of each, and there's no way I'll remember the precise OID everything is at even a week later. I'm adding an object to each command that prints a reminder. This gives me a MIB much like this.

.1.3.6.1.3.2.1 = *no output,*
    top-level OID for firewall state table size group
.1.3.6.1.3.2.1.1 = *the string "firewall state table size"*
.1.3.6.1.3.2.1.2 = *an integer of the state table size*
.1.3.6.1.3.2.2 = *no output, top-level OID for /tmp/appstatus contents*
.1.3.6.1.3.2.2.1 = *the string "contents of /tmp/appstatus"*
.1.3.6.1.3.2.2.2 = *a string containing the first line of /tmp/appstatus*

Now that we know what we're making, let's learn how to get there.

Passthrough Script Input

Snmpd uses arguments to inform the passthrough script of the type of SNMP request, the OID being invoked, and any detail for the request type. I will place my script in `/scripts/pass.sh`, but you should use your host's standard script directory.

```
passthrough-script <flag> <OID> <operation-specific detail>
```

A GET request uses a -g flag. It provides the complete numerical OID, and no operation-specific detail. As with any GET request, the OID must be exact.

```
/scripts/pass.sh -g .1.3.6.1.2.1.1
```

A GETNEXT request uses a −n flag. It passes the complete numerical OID, just like a GET request, and no operation-specific detail.

```
/scripts/pass.sh -n .1.3.6.1.2
```

A SET request uses a −s flag, and passes the complete numerical OID. It also sends the OID type and the contents of the SET request.

```
/scripts/pass.sh -s .1.3.6.1.2.3.0 string "oops"
```

Now that you know what's coming in, let's discuss what comes out.

Passthrough Script Output

The output of your script depends on the SNMP request type.

A GET request for an OID that exists must return three lines. The first line is the requested OID. The second line is the type of OID: integer, string, and so on. The third is the contents of that OID. Here I'm doing a GET on .1.3.6.1.3.2.2.1, one of the OIDs I decided would remind me of my script's functions.

```
$ /scripts/pass.sh -g .1.3.6.1.3.2.2.1
.1.3.6.1.3.2.2.1
string
application state from /tmp/appstatus
```

We have the requested OID, the OID type (string), and the object value.

A GET on a nonexistent OID must return silently.

A GETNEXT also returns three lines. The first line is the next valid OID after the OID you requested. The second line is the next OID's type, and the third is the value of that OID. The output's identical to that for the GET command, except it outputs the next valid object after the one requested. Here I do a GETNEXT on the same OID.

```
$ /scripts/pass.sh -n .1.3.6.1.3.2.2.1
.1.3.6.1.3.2.2.2
string
ok
```

I requested an existing OID, but as the -n makes it a GETNEXT request, we get the next valid object.

The script ignores SET requests, so it should run silently.

Passthrough Script

Given these requirements, we can write a passthrough script. Here's an example, *pass.sh*. It's a simplified derivative of the net-snmp demonstration passthrough script. You can get a copy online at this book's entry at https://mwl.io.

```
#!/bin/sh
#passthrough snmpd extension

ROOTOID=".1.3.6.1.3.2"

SNMPTYPE="$1"
OIDIN="$2"
#OIDOUT is the OID we will return,
#!= REQUESTEDOID if GETNEXT

# handle SET and bail
if  [ "$SNMPTYPE" = "-s" ]; then
   printf "not-writable\n"
   exit 0
# determine OIDOUT for GETNEXT
# next valid OID AFTER the one requested
elif [ "$SNMPTYPE" = "-n" ]; then
   case "$OIDIN" in
   #these are before first OID, 1.1
   $ROOTOID | \
   $ROOTOID.0 | \
   $ROOTOID.0.* | \
   $ROOTOID.1 )
      OIDOUT=$ROOTOID.1.1
      ;;
   #the first OID and later must return second OID
   $ROOTOID.1.1 | \
   $ROOTOID.1.1.* )
      OIDOUT=$ROOTOID.1.2
      ;;
   #the second OID and later must return third OID
   $ROOTOID.1.2 | \
```

```
   $ROOTOID.1.2.* | \
   $ROOTOID.2 )
      OIDOUT=$ROOTOID.2.1
      ;;
   #the third OID and later must return the fourth OID
   $ROOTOID.2.1 | \
   $ROOTOID.2.1.*)
      OIDOUT=$ROOTOID.2.2
      ;;
   #we got handed an OID this script doesn't do
   *)
      logger "GETNEXT received with $*"
      exit 0
      ;;
   esac
elif [ "$SNMPTYPE" = "-g" ]; then
   #It's not a SET or GETNEXT, must be a GET
   #Make sure we didn't pass garbage here
   case "$OIDIN" in
   $ROOTOID.1.1 | \
   $ROOTOID.1.2 | \
   $ROOTOID.2.1 | \
   $ROOTOID.2.2)
      OIDOUT=$OIDIN
      ;;
   *)
      # Drop silently.
      # We don't want to know about every daft typo.
      exit 0
   esac
else
   logger "Unexpected SNMPTYPE with $*"
   exit 0
fi

echo "$OIDOUT"
#figure out what we're supposed to do, and do it

case "$OIDOUT" in
$ROOTOID.1.1)
   printf "string\n"
   printf "firewall state table size\n"
   ;;
$ROOTOID.1.2)
```

```
    printf "integer\n"
    #BSD
    if type pfctl > /dev/null; then
      if STATES=$(pfctl -ss 2> /dev/null); then
    echo $STATES | wc -l | awk '{print $1}'

      else
      printf "-1\n"

        fi
    #Linux
    elif type conntrack > /dev/null; then
      if STATES=$(conntrack -L 2> /dev/null); then
    echo $STATES | wc -l | awk '{print $1}'

      else
      printf "-1\n"

        fi
    fi
    ;;
$ROOTOID.2.1)
    printf "string\n"
    printf "application state from /tmp/appstatus\n"
    ;;
$ROOTOID.2.2)
    printf "string\n"
    if [ -r /tmp/appstatus -a $(wc -l /tmp/appstatus \
       | awk '{print $1}') -gt 0 ]; then
      head -1 /tmp/appstatus
    else
      printf "unknown\n"
    fi
    ;;
*)
    logger "Reached invalid OID at end with $*"
    printf "string\n"
    printf "All Hail Nyarlathotep!\n"
    ;;
esac
exit 0
```

Copy this script to a standard location. Verify that the user running snmpd has all the rights needed to run the script and every program it calls.

Configuring the Passthrough Script

Set up the passthrough script in `snmpd.conf` by using the *pass* keyword, the top OID, and the full path to the script. Here I connect my script `pass.sh` to the OID .1.3.6.1.3.2.

```
pass .1.3.6.1.3.2 /scripts/pass.sh
```

Restart snmpd, and it should be available. Test it with snmpbulkwalk.

```
$ snmpbulkwalk appserver1 .1.3.6.1.3
SNMPv2-SMI::experimental.2.1.1 =
     STRING: "firewall state table size"
SNMPv2-SMI::experimental.2.1.2 = INTEGER: 17
SNMPv2-SMI::experimental.2.2.1 =
     STRING: "application state from /tmp/appstatus"
SNMPv2-SMI::experimental.2.2.2 = STRING: "ok"
```

If you run a complete snmpbulkwalk, these experimental objects should appear in the output.

Debugging the Passthrough Script

The list of things that work correctly on the first try is vanishingly small, and your passthrough script is not on it. You'll need to debug your script.

If you can do an snmpget on individual OIDs, but an snmpbulkwalk doesn't work? You broke the GETNEXT part of your script. Run some snmpgetnext commands to track down which exact OIDs are not returning the proper (meaning the next) OID. You probably confused which OIDs should be next, or which OIDs could be input. Working with raw OIDs bewilders even the experienced.

If you can't do an snmpget on individual OIDs, you could have broken the script literally anywhere else.

Start by running the script at the command line, using the arguments you think it should have. Read the output carefully. The output must be exactly three lines, and must exactly conform to what snmpd expects. Did you leave any debugging in place? Any stray `sh -x` or `echo` statements? White space where it shouldn't be?

If you're on CentOS, check your SELinux logs. This isn't a book on debugging SELinux so I'm not going to take you through the details, but if you're running CentOS you already know how to debug SELinux.[32]

If nothing obvious jumps out, run snmpd in debugging mode. Tell snmpd to stay in the foreground with `-f`. Use `-Le` to spill all output to standard error. Turn on debugging with the `-D` flag, and specify the `ucd-snmp/pass` module.

snmpd -f -Le -Ducd-snmp/pass

Run some more queries. You'll see exactly what command snmpd is running.

```
ucd-snmp/pass: pass-running:  /scripts/pass.sh -n .1.3.6.1.3.2
ucd-snmp/pass: pass-running:  /scripts/pass.sh -n .1.3.6.1.3.2
ucd-snmp/pass: pass-running:  /scripts/pass.sh -n .1.3.6.1.3.2.1.1
...
```

Is snmpd running the same command you are? Did you add an extra dot-whatever in your command line? Copy and paste the command in your terminal to run it manually.

After this, fall back on your regular shell script debugging toolkits. And double-check those OIDs.

Extending Further

The *extend* and *pass* keywords are not the only option for extending SNMP. The antediluvian *exec* and *sh* options still exist, though they're deprecated and should not be used on new installations. If your script needs better performance, or takes too long to run, consider using a standalone daemon using *pass_persist*.

---

32   I tried writing a passthrough script to disable SELinux via SNMP, but it turns out you have to configure SELinux to permit the script to run from SNMP, which rather ruins the point.

With *pass_persist*, your extension program keeps running. The agent starts your program when it starts and terminates it when snmpd exits. If you can already write daemons in any language, and you understand passthrough scripts, writing a *pass_persist* daemon isn't hard. Most languages have *pass_persist* libraries.

For greater efficiency, consider writing an SNMP subagent and connecting it to snmpd with AgentX. At that point, you're in the big time.

Net-snmp Subagents

The big problem with extensions is that the agent blocks until the extension command finishes. Snmpd won't respond to other requests until the *pass* command completes. You don't want your network management system to report that the host isn't responding to queries about network throughput while your custom command runs.

Cope with blocking net-snmp modules by moving them into one or more AgentX subagents. The master agent and each subagent are separate processes, returning in their own time. A single bulkwalk will experience delays as the slow modules run, but queries from other managers or processes will proceed normally. While many sysadmins have an instinct to proactively configure software to avoid the problems we think will happen, don't proactively move big chunks of snmpd into running as a subagent. Net-snmp's snmpd isn't really designed to be split up into many tiny chunks. Only configure snmpd as a subagent once you experience trouble. Subagents are complicated. Complication causes outages.

While it's possible to put any number of modules into a subagent, we'll focus on the problematic passthrough modules.

Subagent Module Selection

The snmpd modules that should go into a subagent depend entirely on your host and what you're using it for. A host serving as a multi-peer BGP border router, with big long IP forwarding tables, might benefit from having the routing modules as a subagent. If you have extended the agent as per Chapter 10 and the commands take a long time to complete, put the extensions in a subagent.

Start with the list of modules compiled into your snmpd, as discussed in Chapter 1. Find the modules that support the feature you want to move into a sub-agent. Start with the `snmpd.conf` keywords. Extend snmpd's features with the keywords *pass*, *pass_persist*, *extend*, *exec*, *execfix*, and *extendfix*. Check the file `module.list` we generated for anything like those keywords.

```
$ grep -E "pass|extend|exec" modules.list
ucd-snmp/pass
ucd-snmp/pass_persist
agent/extend
utilities/execute
ucd-snmp/pass_common
```

There's modules named *pass*, *pass_persist*, and *extend*. There's also a *pass_common* module, which from the name alone looks suspiciously like it might be shared functions for the first two modules. Net-snmp likes shared modules, but how do we verify that? Internet searches uncover several discussions that say it is, so I'll add *pass_common* to my list. There's an *extend* module, so that's another keyword. But what about *exec*, *execfix*, and *extendfix*? There's a *utilities/execute* module, but we can't be certain that's the same.

I find the snmpd source code and grep(1) useful. Each module has its own source file, usually named after the module. If you can identify the file where a keyword is defined, that's a good hint that it's part of that module. I've extracted the net-snmp 5.8 software into my home directory. Search the snmpd source code for each of these.

```
$ cd net-snmp-5.8/agent/
$ grep -Rw extendfix *
mibgroup/agent/extend.c:    snmpd_register_config_handler
("extendfix", extend_parse_config, NULL, NULL);
mibgroup/agent/extend.c:        !strcmp( token, "extendfix"
) ||
```

This file `mibgroup/agent/extend.c` defines the *extendfix* keyword. It's part of the module *extend*. Similar searches on *exec* and *execfix* show that they are in the files `mibgroup/agent/extend.c` and `mibgroup/utilities/execute.c`, so we need both the *extend* and *execute* modules.

The complete list of modules we need is: *pass*, *pass_persist*, *pass_common*, *extend*, and *execute*. These modules will be disabled in the master agent, and will be the only modules run inside the subagent.

Subagent Configuration Files

Each instance of snmpd needs its own configuration files, and can only understand the configuration statements for the modules it has loaded. In our example the master agent can't parse any *pass* statements, while the subagent can't understand keywords like *syscontact*, *proc*, and any authentication configuration.

I recommend naming the agent configuration file after the agent's role. File names like `snmpd.master.conf` and `snmpd.pass.conf` are unmistakable.

The persistent data file complicates everything, though. Each instance of snmpd expects complete control over the persistent data files, and only writes data that it understands to those files. If multiple snmpd processes compete for the same file, it doesn't matter which one wins. You will lose. Lose persistent data, that is. Seeing as that data includes your SNMPv3 users, this would be bad. You must assign each snmpd instance its own persistent data directory. I recommend using a subdirectory of your operating system's default persistent data directory. If your persistent data directory is `/var/net-snmp`, I would create subdirectories like `/var/net-snmp/master`, `/var/net-snmp/pass`, and so on. Don't let any snmpd instance use the default persistent data directory; that way, if an `snmpd.conf` appears in that directory you'll know that something is misconfigured.

The snmp_config(5) man page shows several ways to set the persistent directory. Three of them are environment variables, which are tricky to manage with several similar processes. One is the catch-all default. The last is the *persistentDir* configuration file option—but it's for `snmp.conf`, not `snmpd.conf`. You can tell a manager where to find persistent data, but can't tell the agent where to put it?

Don't beat your head against the brick wall, there's a solution.

Most net-snmp configuration keywords only work in a specific frame of reference. Some configure `snmpd`, some set up managers like `snmpbulkwalk`. You wouldn't want to set a listening address for snmpset any more than you'd set a single default username for snmpd. Net-snmp allows you to use keywords in different frames of reference, specifically letting you work around edge cases like this.

Use `[snmp]` in a configuration file to declare that you're using an `snmp.conf` keyword normally used to configure managers. Similarly, use `[snmpd]` to indicate that you're switching to `snmpd.conf` keywords normally used for agents. This lets you effectively set up an `snmpd.conf` for the master agent and each subagent, but include a little snippet of `snmp.conf` to be used just for that agent. We'll use the *persistentDir* keyword and `[snmp]` as an example.

On a line by itself, these bracketed keywords mean "everything that follows is from this frame of reference, until another bracketed keyword switches us back." Use this format if you need multiple alien keywords.

Here I have a snippet of `snmpd.conf`. The *agentaddress* keyword is a usual `snmpd.conf` keyword. We use `[snmp]` to switch to `snmp.conf` keywords, defining the persistent data directory. Once we've finished with that, we use `[snmpd]` to revert to *snmpd.conf* keywords, and tell this agent it's a master agent.

```
...
agentaddress udp6::161
[snmp]
persistentDir /var/net-snmp/master/
[snmpd]
master agentx
```

If an alien keyword shares a line with the bracketed marker, it means that the context change applies only to this line.

```
...
agentaddress udp6::161
[snmp] persistentDir /var/net-snmp/master/
master agentx
```

This agent will now use the persistent data directory */var/net-snmp/master*.

The master agent configuration file needs the *master agentx* keyword. The subagent needs only the options for the modules it understands, such as *pass* and *exec* statements. You'll tell the subagent it's a subagent with a command-line option.

Running Agents and Subagents

Write a shell script to start your agents. Integrate this script into your host's init scripts. Individual Unixes have their own styles for startup and shutdown scripts, so I won't make this example fit any particular one. I will discuss the command line options for each type of agent.

Each snmpd process needs its own configuration files, and should not read any files used by other snmpd instances. Use the -C command-line option to tell snmpd to not read any configuration files other than those specified, and -c to provide a comma-delimited list of configuration files it should read.

The -p flag lets you specify a pidfile for this process. Use a pidfile that contains the agent's role, like *snmpd.master.pid* or *snmpd.pass.pid*.

Use -I to provide a list of modules that the agent should initialize. Use this list to tell the subagent what it gets. If that list starts with a minus sign, it's the list of modules that the agent will *not* initialize. On the master agent, use the same list you used for the subagent, but with the minus sign so it won't start the modules in the subagent.

Finally, use -X to tell your subagent that it's running as a subagent. This option makes it seek out its master.

All together, we have a startup script like this.

```
#!/bin/sh

PASS="pass,pass_persist,pass_common,extend,execute"

echo "Starting master agent"
/usr/sbin/snmpd -C \
    -c /etc/snmp/snmpd.master.conf,/var/net-snmp/master/snmpd.conf \
    -p /var/run/snmpd.master.pid -I -$PASS

echo "Starting pass subagent"
/usr /sbin/snmpd -C \
    -c /etc/snmp/snmpd.pass.conf,/var/net-snmp/pass/snmpd.conf \
    -p /var/run/snmpd.pass.pid -X -I $PASS
```

First we define a variable, *PASS*, that lists all the modules that we want to delegate to the subagent.

Starting our master agent means discarding all the standard configuration files with -C, then reading in both our regular and persistent configuration files with -c. We define a pid file with -p. Finally, list the modules we don't want the master to start. Note the "-" in front of the module list, turning them off.

Starting the subagent is very similar. It uses a different pidfile and different configuration files. We add -X so that this instance of snmpd knows it's a subagent. Finally, we list the modules that we want the subagent to initialize. It's the same list that the master agent *shouldn't* initialize.

The agent shutdown script is simple.

```
#!/bin/sh
echo "sacrificing children"
pkill -F /var/run/snmpd.pass.pid

echo "sacrificing parent"
pkill -F /var/run/snmpd.master.pid
```

If your Unix shuts down processes some other way, be certain you use the TERM signal to shut down snmpd so that it will write its persistent data files before shutting down.

Multiple Subagents

On a heavily loaded machine you might find that you must split more than one feature out into a subagent. That's okay. Figure out which modules you must split out and create a new configuration file. The master agent script can accept multiple module variables as arguments to -I, so long as you separate them with commas.

There's a school of thought that says the master agent should have as little as possible running in it, and all the various agent functions should be split out into subagents. I understand the appeal. Net-snmp isn't really written to run in this way, however. Do not overcomplicate things.

Now let's talk about monitoring with SNMP, and some other tools you might not have considered.

Chapter 11: Monitoring

You can now read and write data to SNMP, walk up and down the MIB, extend the net-snmp agent, and scream *knowledgeably* at vendors for their infuriatingly buggy implementations. For many of us, the whole point of using SNMP is to watch our equipment. We touched on monitoring back in the Introduction, with vague platitudes like "don't overload systems with monitoring traffic!" In this chapter, we'll discuss the specifics of monitoring certain aspects of a host for both general SNMP MIBs, and net-snmp-specific expansions.

Management systems always know how to monitor network traffic. Beyond that, any monitoring almost certainly requires a human being deciding which system characteristics need watching.

Most information useful for monitoring appears in tables. You'll look at a table, see an interesting column, and decide to monitor it. You need the specific OID to monitor an entry. Get the full OID name and number by running `snmptranslate -Td -Ib` **`columnname`**. Read that description to verify it does what you think it does, then walk that object to see what's really in there. Chapter 3 discusses getting specific OIDs from tables.

This chapter presents a bunch of different ways to view information. You can't monitor everything, so which of them should you use? I can't tell you. Every environment and application is different. No matter which monitoring tool or protocol you use, monitoring target selection always comes down to "make your best guess and hope."

Gauges and Counters

A huge source of confusion in monitoring with SNMP is the difference between *gauge* and *counter* object types. Most network management systems will automatically use the correct type for common objects, but if you have to leave those comfortable MIBs and trek out into the uncharted realms previously beyond humanity's reach, you must configure these yourself.

A *gauge* is like a speedometer. It provides insight into what's happening at this precise second. At a restaurant, it's how many hamburgers are being eaten at this instant. This seems like it would be the obvious measure to use for almost everything, but not everything can be measured so exactly. For sufficiently fine values of "this instant," each processor is handling exactly one task: the task of reporting how many tasks are running on the processor. A network card is either handling a packet, or it's not.

A *counter* is like an odometer, measuring how much of something has been processed. It's how many hamburgers the restaurant has served in its existence. We measure traffic across a network interface by counting how many bytes have passed through the interface. The network management system computes running averages by subtracting the last value from the current value and dividing by the time.

I'd like to offer rules for when each gets used, except I can't. Counters are great for measuring wildly fluctuating data like network traffic, except when they aren't. Use gauges to measure steadier data, except when you can't. Both data types are attempts to map a wildly erratic physical world into nice clean data. SNMP MIB developers have two choices for how to display such numerical data, and pick the least awful one.

We lowly SNMP users must be aware that the data can be in two types, and configure our systems to use the correct data. If your monitoring system produces nonsensical graphs for an object, verify that it's using the correct type. If your graph goes into negative numbers, you're processing a gauge as a counter. If the graph is a series of spikes that drop back towards zero, you're using a counter as a gauge. Incomprehensible graphs could be either, or perhaps a buggy agent, an NMS bug, or an object you should have never tried to graph in the first place.

The Network

Modern SNMP includes a whole bunch of networking MIBs. Every management system knows how to measure throughput. Let's discuss interfaces and routing.

Interface Statistics

The SNMP table `ifXTable` contains a bunch of objects specifically for monitoring modern network interfaces. This MIB uses 64-bit counters, which in a network traffic context means that they roll over after about eighteen exabytes of traffic.

Run `snmptable -Cbw 100 `**`hostname`**` ifXTable` and take a look. Adjust the `100` to fit the size of your terminal and we'll consider a few of the more useful entries.

The `ifHCInOctets` and `ifHCOutOctets` objects are the standard "how much traffic has passed through this interface." You can measure unicast traffic with `ifHCInUcastPkts` and `ifHCOutUcastPkts`, multicast with `ifHCInMulticastPkts` and `ifHCOutMulticastPkts`, and broadcast with `ifHCInBroadcastPkts` and `ifHCOutBroadcastPkts`.

The `HighSpeed` entry gives the interface's current speed, as negotiated with the switch, in megabits per second. Your average gigabit interface shows up as 1000. It does not show the actual traffic that the interface can support—I've seen more than one "gigabit" card that chokes trying to pass a hundred megabit. If you want to verify that a card is correctly autonegotiating with the switch, monitor this.[33] Virtual interfaces

---

[33] Hard-coding interface speeds was useful for hundred megabit connections between certain vendors with infuriatingly incompatible autonegotiation implementations, but gigabit and faster connections autonegotiate vital characteristics other than speed and duplex. Disable autonegotiation at your peril.

can show up as gigabit or even ten gig, but might be even faster.

The `PromiscuousMode` object tells if an interface is in promiscuous mode. Many security-sensitive organizations have controls on promiscuous interfaces, and monitoring this object can help support those controls.

`ConnectorPresent` supposedly tells you if there's a connector on the physical interface. It's for devices with SPFs, GBICs, and other removable connectors. Your typical RJ45 network card always has a connector present. (Technically it's an 8-pin, 8-conductor receptacle but, like everything else in computing, we call it a connector for historical reasons.)

ifTable and Monitoring

The older `ifTable` uses 32-bit counters and gauges and is not suited for measuring throughput on gigabit or faster interfaces. These counters can roll over every 4.29 gigabytes of traffic, which means that for accurate queries you must query gigabit interfaces every forty seconds and ten-gigabit interfaces every four seconds. Some network management systems still use the objects in `ifTable`, though. If you find your NMS querying these old objects for throughput, you need a new NMS.

The `ifInDiscards` and `ifInErrors` columns are also 32 bits. Interface errors are important but rare. Is detecting them worth the monitoring resources? Copper gets errors almost by definition, but fiber links shouldn't. I err on the side of monitoring them, because I would rather demand more resources from my employers than explain to them why I didn't catch the error. Save the email where your boss rejects the request; it might not save you from being sacrificed on the Altar of Accountability after the inevitable disaster, but you'll at least have the pleasure of saying, "I told you so." Similarly, you can monitor discarded frames and if an interface is up or down.

Or you might be happier not knowing exactly how trash your equipment is.

IP Addresses

We don't generally monitor a host's IP addresses, but the ability to grab them via scripts is highly useful for system management.

The current standard way to grab IP addresses from an agent is the protocol-independent `ipAddressTable`. Not all agents have implemented this table, though, so you might have to use the older `ipAddrTable` for IPv4 addresses and `ipv6AddrTable` for IPv6. Use `snmptable -Cbiw 100` *hostname* `ipAddressTable`, adjusting the `100` to your terminal width.

If the IPv6 address table displays illegibly, try adding the `-OX` flag to make the output imitate an array-style index format.

Routing Tables

Monitoring routing tables is usually pointless on servers, but often useful for routers. `IP-FORWARD-MIB` contains several objects useful for route monitoring. You'll see two versions, some containing the word *inet* and others containing *ip*.

The objects in `ipCidrRouteTable`, all beginning with *ip*, predate IPv6. If all else fails, just about every agent supports these objects. Only use them if you must. Some information is not available in `ipCidrRouteTable`.

The newer *inet* objects support both IPv4 and IPv6. Most of them are in the table `inetCidrRouteTable`, but there are a couple of useful objects outside the table. A surprising number of organizations, including a number of "minimal viable product" router manufacturers, have not implemented `inetCidrRouteTable` in their devices.

One common monitoring subject is the number of routes in the agent's routing table. The OID `IP-FORWARD-MIB::inetCidrRouteNumber.0` gives the total number of routes, including both IPv4 and IPv6. Some but not all older devices offer `IP-FORWARD-MIB::ipCidrRouteTable.0` as an equivalent. If nothing else, you can always walk the table and count.

If you're monitoring the routing table, chances are you don't routinely care about the contents of that table. What concerns you is the number of valid routes that get thrown away. Discarded valid routes mean that the router is short on memory, or something even worse is wrong. Monitor `IP-FORWARD-MIB::inetCidrRouteDiscards.0` to see if your routers start throwing routes away.

If you want to pull the entire routing table, grab `inetCidrRouteTable` or `ipCidrRouteTable`. Pulling the entire route table with SNMP is much like pulling it on the command line. Those of you who run heavily loaded border routers with multiple BGP peers and internal OSPF should be just as leery of pulling the whole routing table via SNMP as you are running `show ip route` on an overburdened Cisco's command line.

Any time you go near the routing table, be *absolutely certain* to use snmpbulkwalk(1) rather than snmpwalk(1). A default bulk walk grabs ten entries per request, so it literally takes approximately one tenth the time as a crufty old snmpwalk. You might increase the number of repeaters, so that each request grabs even more information. I find using forty repeaters (`-Cr40`) to collect forty objects per request usually returns routing tables without packet fragmentation.

If you're in any doubt, use snmpnetstat(1).

Interactive Network Assessment: snmpnetstat

SNMP might give you quick access to a host's network information, but remembering which hosts support which tables, which are indexed well, and which need special flags is annoying. The snmpnetstat(1) command handles all this for you, at the cost of remembering which command-line flag represents which information. If a host doesn't support a modern table, or bulk requests, it automatically falls back until it finds one that works.

Use snmpnetstat to view open sockets and live connections, network interface details, protocol statistics, and the routing table. All of these functions can be done from a terminal on the remote host. Personally, I'm too lazy to bother SSHing into a server just to run a single command when snmpnetstat will do it for me.

To disable DNS resolution on any of these commands, add the -Cn flag.

Live Connections

By default, snmpnetstat shows only the current connections on a host. Here I ask my web server to tell me how busy it is.

```
$ snmpnetstat www
Active Internet (tcp) Connections
Proto Local Address      Remote Address            State    PID
tcp4  www.mwl.io.http    31.193.51.74.46125        TIMEWAIT   0
tcp4  www.mwl.io.http    broadband.actcorp..3073   ESTABLISHED 0
tcp4  www.mwl.io.https   broadband.actcorp..3081   ESTABLISHED 0
tcp4  www.mwl.io.https   ip-54-36-150-153.a.25228  ESTABLISHED 0
tcp6  www.mwl.io.https   broadband.bt.com.64597    FINWAIT2   0
...
```

What I don't see are open server sockets. Add -Ca to get those. That will add a section like this.

```
$ snmpnetstat -Ca www
Active Internet (tcp) Connections
Proto Local Address      Remote Address            State    PID
...
Listening Internet (tcp) Connections
Proto Local Address      PID
tcp4  *.smtp             0
tcp4  *.http             0
...
```

The -Cf flag lets you choose an address family. Use -Cf inet to display only IPv4, or -Cf inet6 for IPv6.

The -Cp flag lets you show only one protocol, as named in /etc/protocols. You can use -Cp tcp to only show TCP connections, -Cp udp for UDP, or any other name.[34]

---

34   You cannot use a protocol number as in /etc/protocols, but only a few nutjobs like myself know about those, so that's okay.

Network Interfaces

To get a summary of all network interfaces, use -Ci. This shows useful information like errors, IP address, and so on.

```
$ snmpnetstat -Ci www
Name       Mtu Network      Address       Ipkts  Ierrs  Opkts Oerrs Queue
vtnet0    1500 192.0.2/24   192.0.2.193   364906     0 266030     0     0
loo      16384 127/8        127.0.0.1     216209     0 216076     0     0
```

To see dropped packets in this table, use -Cid. To add bytes passed in and out, add -Cb. If you're querying a device that uses a byte that isn't eight bits, use -Co instead.

If you're only interested in a single interface, specify it with -CI.

```
$ snmpnetstat -CI vtnet0 www
```

You can also view an interface's characteristics in near real time by specifying an interface name and an interval. Use -CI to give an interface name, and -Cw to specify a number of seconds between updates. The results won't appear until after the first interval passes. I'm suspicious that my server's interface vtnet0 might be dropping packets right now, so I check.

```
$ snmpnetstat -CdI vtnet0 -Cw 5 www
            input         vtnet0              output
  packets  errs      bytes  packets  errs      bytes colls drops
       12     0       1089        7     0       1233     0     0
       78     0       5656       31     0      79668     0     0
       54     0       2041       23     0      72539     0     0
...
```

The drop column isn't increasing, so whatever's wrong isn't discarded packets or interface errors. Hit CTRL-C to interrupt the display.

Protocol Statistics

Get the host's TCP/IP protocol statistics with the -Cs flag. Use -Css to hide everything equal to zero.

```
$ snmpnetstat -Css www
tcp:
        1283089 active opens
        2255116 passive opens
            300 failed attempts
         757338 resets of established connections
...
```

This is exactly like running `netstat -s` and `netstat -ss` on the host.

Routing Table

View the host's routing table with the `-Cr` flag. I don't want to delay my results for a bunch of DNS lookups that I know won't return anything, so I add the `-Cn` flag.

```
$ snmpnetstat -Crn gwtest
Routing tables (ipCidrRouteTable)
Destination        Gateway            Flags    Interface
default            69.14.191.65       <UG>     ether1-wow
69.14.191.64/27    69.14.191.73       <U>      ether1-wow
203.0.113.1/24     203.0.113.1        <U>      bridge
...
```

Note that snmpnetstat shows you which table it took the information from. This so-called router isn't offering modern SNMP routing tables.

I could add the `-Cf` flags and specify `inet` (only IPv4) or `inet6` (only IPv6) to narrow my request as needed.

You should not need to log into a host just to check network information ever again.

Disk Capacity

Full disks cause outages. We're accustomed to thinking of disks as server things, but embedded devices also have onboard storage. A router with a full flash drive can be just as balky as a server without space to put its logs. SNMP's HOST-RESOURCES-MIB contains objects specifically for monitoring storage. They haven't changed a huge amount over time, because while the numbers have gotten bigger the general concepts of disks haven't changed since the 1990s. Most storage information appears under `hrStorageTable`. (Net-snmp's snmpd contains special features to alarm on preconfigured storage errors, but we'll consider those separately.) Look at your test host's table by running `snmptable -Cw 100 ` **`hostname`** ` hrStorageTable` and follow along, adjusting the `100` for your terminal width.

The `hrStorageIndex` column is notable because it's not sequential. Your operating system presents storage devices with its own inscrutable naming system, and snmpd rides along with it.

The `hrStorageType` column tells you which sort of storage the line represents, and which MIB defines it. They're overwhelmingly defined in `HOST-RESOURCES-TYPES`, and you can usually figure out what sort it is from the type name. Doing so is unnecessary, because the `hrStorageDescr` column gives you either a description like "Physical memory," "Cached memory," or a partition mount point. Yes, SNMP considers physical memory a storage device. You can monitor RAM as storage, although SNMP has better MIBs for doing so.

`hrStorageAllocationUnits` tells us what size of storage block snmpd claims that the disk uses. Most modern disks use 4096 byte (4K) blocks, though you'll find plenty of older devices that use 512-byte blocks. All storage information is given in this unit. The catch with `hrStorageAllocationUnits` is that many agents find it necessary to lie. The maximum number of blocks on a disk is a 32-bit counter. Large filesystems can exceed that. To make the numbers work, snmpd and many other agents adjust the value of `hrStorageAllocation` as needed to make the numbers fit. The proportions are correct. The final amount of disk space used and free are correct. The block size is a lie.[35]

The `hrStorageSize` column shows the size of the disk, in units defined by `hrStorageAllocationUnits`. Multiply this by `hrStorageAllocationUnits` to get the actual size.

---

35   Here, snmpd participates in an esteemed tradition of storage devices that not only lie, they stack lies atop one another.

hrStorageUsed gives the number of storage units used on this disk. Multiply it by hrStorageAllocationUnits to get the actual amount of space used.

Lastly, hrStorageAllocationFailures shows how many write requests were rejected because the disk was full.

To monitor a disk, you'll use hrStorageAllocationUnits to get the disk size and hrStorageUsed to get the current utilization. This generates a valid graph of proportional usage, but might have incorrect units. When you configure monitoring, I encourage telling your NMS to use the block size from hrStorageAllocationUnits to generate graphs that have actual, correct disk sizes.

Understand what each storage device is before trying to monitor it. Many storage devices are ephemeral, and should not be monitored. Notably, systemd creates and destroys mount points as it needs. Monitoring all those mount points is not productive. There are better objects to use for memory tracking, as we'll see later.

NFS Monitoring

Snmpd has a couple of options to adjust how it presents network file systems. If you must monitor NFS shares as mounted on the clients, consider these before you start.

Net-snmp's agent does not show NFS shares mounted on a client by default. If you want to show NFS mounts in the client's storage table, set the option *skipNFSInHostResources* to *false*.

If you are showing NFS mounts on the client, they normally show up as "Fixed Disks." That's how net-snmp first implemented the support. The standard later declared such disks should show up as "Network Disks." If you want to follow the standard, set *storageUseNFS* to *1*.

Excluding Disk Devices

If you know a disk is having trouble, don't poke at it. While the proper solution is to fix the blasted storage device, you can sometimes patch around it with the *ignoredisk* directive.

```
ignoredisk /dev/ada0
```

The problem with *ignoredisk* is that it only works when you're mapping actual disk devices. Folks running storage system middleware like ZFS or Linux device mappers can't successfully use it. The good news is, the function of middleware layers like ZFS is to obscure lower level errors from the users and applications. Users shouldn't notice lower level problems. You must monitor these errors through some other mechanism, though. What mechanism? That depends entirely on your middleware. But the middleware won't otherwise interfere with your disk utilization tracking and alarming.

Disk Input and Output

While how much space in a partition remains free is an important number, so is how much the disk gets read from and written to. A disk that remains pretty much half full but gets millions of read and write requests a minute has a problem very different from, but just as serious as, a full disk. Net-snmp includes `diskIOTable` to provide per-disk I/O information. This goes beneath the partition-based information in `hrStorageTable` to access the raw disk statistics. Run `snmptable hostname diskIOTable` and follow along.

The *diskIODevice* column shows the disk device beneath */dev*. Some of these will be disk-like devices that aren't really for storage, such as */dev/dm-0* on CentOS or */dev/pass* devices on FreeBSD. You should recognize actual storage devices such as */dev/sda*, */dev/sr0*, and */dev/ada0*.

The `diskIONRead` and `diskIONWritten` columns show the number of bytes read from and written to the disk device since boot. These are 32-bit counters, and can overflow comparatively quickly. For truly busy disks checked rarely, you'll need the 64-bit counters of `diskIONReadX` and `diskIONWrittenX` at the end of the table. Most of us do just fine using the 32-bit counters, however, and only need the 64-bit counters as sanity checks during debugging.

The `diskIOReads` and `diskIOWrites` gives the number of read and write accesses since boot.

The `diskIOLA1`, `diskIOLA5`, and `diskIOLA15` columns give the percent of time the disk was busy over one, five, and fifteen minutes.

Monitoring I/O makes no sense for pseudodevices like virtual mounts, null mounts, loopback mounts, memory file systems, and so on. Linux versions of snmpd include the options *diskio_exclude_ram* and *diskio_exclude_loop* to not include these devices in the disk I/O table. It also has *diskio_exclude_fd* to exclude floppy disks.[36]

Net-SNMP Disk Utilization Alarms

While the monitoring team should be involved in the decision of what to monitor, sometimes the sysadmin knows better than anyone when alarms should trigger. Snmpd includes support for setting alarm levels for full partitions in the agent, allowing the sysadmin to set alarm levels. The management system can walk these objects and look for any values in an alarm state. This feature also provides information not included in `hrStorageTable`.

The table `dskTable` contains only partitions with alarms configured, so we'll start by configuring alarms.

Configuring Disk Space Alarms

Use the *disk* `snmpd.conf` keyword to set an alarm. It takes the path to the filesystem to be monitored, and an amount of minimum free space to alarm at.

```
disk mountpoint <free space>
```

Define the amount of free space either in kilobytes, or in a percentage. You can't use convenient shorthand like 1G; actual space measurements must be in kilobytes. Given the size of modern partitions, I go with a percentage.

---

36   No, I'm not going to make a snarky comment here. Anyone who legitimately uses floppy disks these days has enough problems that they don't need me piling on.

If a Linux `/boot` partition fills up, I can't upgrade the kernel. Here I set snmpd to alarm when `/boot` is less than 10% free.

```
disk  /boot 10%
```

Linux tends to put most everything else on the root partition. Here I configure snmpd to alarm when / is less than 99% free. This is blatantly unreasonable, but I'm deliberately triggering an error so that we have something to look at.

```
disk  / 99%
```

If you want to monitor every single disk at the same level, no matter what sort of disk it is or its function, use the keyword *includeAllDisks* and a percentage. While there's really no reason to monitor `/dev/shm` or `/sys/fs/cgroup`, ignoring these might be easier than configuring individual partition monitoring.

```
includeAllDisks 10%
```

You can override *includeAllDisks* on specific partitions with a separate *disk* entry.

Restart snmpd, and we will have a net-snmp disk table to look at.

The Disk Table

Net-snmp provides all its special disk information in `dskTable`. Note the lack of an "i" here. This is another wide table, so to look at it in its pure form you'll want to use `-Cw` to specify a terminal width. Run `snmptable -Cw 100` **hostname** `dskTable`, adjusting the `100` for the width of your terminal.

Lots of columns here, right? Many of them are not routinely useful. The various `dskTotal`, `dskAvail`, and `dskUsed` columns use multiple 32-bit counters to represent 64-bit values. Don't monitor them. Use the much easier disk size values in `hrStorageTable` instead.

We only care about columns 1, 2, 17, and 18.

The first two columns, `dskIndex` and `dskPath`, show the table index and the partition.

The column `dskErrorFlag` shows if the partition is in an error state or not. This contains either `noError` or `error`.

Finally, the column `dskErrorMessage` contains the error message that your network management system will retrieve.

Perhaps the easiest way to check for errors is to walk the relevant part of the MIB. Here we have one partition without an error, and one with.

```
$ snmpbulkwalk testhost UCD-SNMP-MIB::dskErrorFlag
UCD-SNMP-MIB::dskErrorFlag.1 = INTEGER: noError(0)
UCD-SNMP-MIB::dskErrorFlag.2 = INTEGER: error(1)
```

Checking the error messages shows us the error.

```
$ snmpbulkwalk db1 UCD-SNMP-MIB::dskErrorMsg
UCD-SNMP-MIB::dskErrorMsg.1 = STRING:
UCD-SNMP-MIB::dskErrorMsg.2 =
      STRING: /: less than 99% free (= 88%)
```

The error message contains sufficient information to identify the problem. If your management system has the ability to walk `UCD-SNMP-MIB::dskErrorMsg` and alarm if anything has a value, do so. While the management system should have its own error levels for disk utilization, allowing the sysadmin to set additional errors is not bad.

Interactive Disk Monitoring

Just as with the network, you can use SNMP to interactively check disk utilization. The snmpdf(1) command reads `hrStorageTable` and presents the results in a format familiar to users of df(1). As the table includes a bunch of non-disk stuff, you'll also get entries for different types of memory and swap space and such.

Instead of showing the results in the native blocks, I recommend adding the `-CH` flag to use familiar human-readable measurements.

```
$ snmpdf -CH db1
Description              Size        Used   Available Used%
Physical memory        1.01GB   142.07MB    872.75MB   13%
...
/                      17.81GB     2.12GB    15.69GB   11%
/dev/shm              507.41MB     0.00kB   507.41MB    0%
...
/boot                  1.04GB   165.89MB    872.45MB   15%
...
```

If you add the -Cu flag, snmpdf reads dskTable rather than hrStorageTable, eliminating the memory entries. I find a df-style representation of memory helpful, especially on embedded devices without complicated memory models, to simultaneously examine both disk and memory usage.

Viewing Processes

The host resources MIB provides information on running processes in the table hrSWRunTable. It's not really useful for monitoring, but it's handy if you want to see all the userland and kernel processes running on a host. Depending on your operating system and what's running on your host, this table can be even wider than ifXTable. Run snmptable -Cw 100 *hostname* hrSWRunTable and follow along, adjusting the 100 to fit your terminal.

The first column, hrSWRunIndex, is the process ID. The whole table is indexed by PID. Using numbers as an index is straightforward, but it makes it very hard to identify if a particular process is running or not. This list includes kernel threads. As kernel thread numbering overlaps process IDs, 100,000 is added to the kernel thread ID.

The hrSWRunName column gives the name of the program. It should include details like the version number and organization that wrote it, but in most agents it's just the brief filename of the binary.

The hrSWRunID column gives a product ID, if applicable. It's rarely used today.

Under hrSWRunPath you should get the full path to the program that was executed. Some programs, such as Sendmail, manage to muck this up.

The column `hrSWRunParameters` shows the command-line arguments used to start this program. SNMP does not guarantee that the program is still using these parameters; remember, some programs have external control programs that change their behavior.

The `hrSWRunType` column shows what sort of process this is. Userland programs have a `hrSWRunType` of *application*. Kernel threads use *operatingSystem* or *deviceDriver*. A process that shows up as *unknown* means trouble, but I haven't seen one of these for decades.

Finally, `hrSWRunStatus` shows if the software can be run or not. Some agents allow you to set this "invalid" (4) to kill the software, but snmpd does not.

So how would you check to make sure that, say, sendmail, cron, and httpd were running? Some network management software can parse `hrSWRunTable` and dig out answers. Most of us must use net-snmp specific alarm methods.

Net-SNMP Per-Process Alarms

Since you can't easily grab a single process by OID from the running software table, net-snmp provides a way to set up monitoring on vital processes. An *alarm* is an easily-queried OID whose value indicates the presence or absence of a problem. The table `prTable` includes information on configured processes, limits, and more. Snmpd doesn't populate this table unless you tell it to monitor some processes, so we'll start there.

Configuring Process Alarms

Use the *proc* `snmpd.conf` keyword to set up process alarms. You must provide at least one argument, the process name as shown in `ps -acx`. After that, you can specify numbers of maximum and minimum processes of that type that can be running.

```
proc <process name> <maximum limit> <minimum limit>
```

If you give no limits after the process name, you're declaring that at least one instance of this program must be running. There's no upper limit how many of this process could be running. Here, I expect at least one `httpd` process to be running.

```
proc httpd
```

Not checking maximum counts is foolish, however. Sure, a small server could legitimately have a dozen web server processes running. A big server could have hundreds of them. But there is an upper limit, beyond which there's trouble. My web server normally has about two dozen `httpd` processes running. When someone links to my site from Hacker News or Reddit, though, that can go up to forty or fifty. Running fewer than five would be an error. So here I set an upper limit of sixty, and a lower limit of five.

```
proc httpd 60 5
```

Use this configuration style for daemons with a variable number of processes such as php-fpm, sendmail, squid, and so on.

I use blacklistd(8) to feed spammer IP addresses to my packet filter. This host should always run one, and exactly one, `blacklistd`.

```
proc blacklistd 1 1
```

Use this configuration for daemons that should have a fixed number of processes like `cron`, `syslogd`, and `snmpd`.

If a process should never be running, set its limits to zero. Some intruders like to spoof programs called `systemd`. My production network is systemd-free. If a process of that name appears on one of my hosts without systemd, I have a problem.

```
proc systemd 0 0
```

If you have an upper limit on the number of a process that can run, but no lower limit, specify only the upper limit. If my regularly scheduled newsyslog(8) job runs long enough to overlap the next scheduled run, I must investigate.

```
proc newsyslog 1
```

Use this to alarm on maintenance jobs that run irregularly.

Restart snmpd to make the process table available.

Process Status Table

The table `prTable` contains all configured process alarms. Here's part of the table on one of my webservers.

```
$ snmptable -Cb www prtable
SNMP table: UCD-SNMP-MIB::prTable
```

Index	Names	Min	Max	Count	ErrorFlag	ErrMessage	ErrFix	ErrFixCmd
1	httpd	5	60	11	noError		noError	
2	php-fpm	3	10	4	noError		noError	
3	memcached	1	1	1	noError		noError	
4	sshd	2	10	5	noError		noError	

The `prNames` column shows the name of the process to be monitored, as configured in *snmpd.conf*.

Under `prMin` and `prMax`, we get the maximum and minimum limits on how many of this process is permitted.

The `prCount` field is how many processes with this name are actually running. This column has no indication if the number here triggers an error state or not. It's the raw data used to make that determination, however.

The `prErrorFlag` field indicates if there's an error. A value of *noError* means that we're in the permitted range. If it says *error*, there's an additional message saying if there's too many or too few of the process. It's only measured when you query the object.

The `prErrFix` and `prErrFixCmd` columns are used if you want to use SET commands to attempt to fix these errors. Many management systems have their own preferred ways to attempt to fix errors, so we're not going to cover these. Look at the *procfix* keyword in the *snmpd.conf* manual page if this feature intrigues you.

Memory and Swap

A system that runs out of memory is in trouble. A system that exhausts its memory and swap space is in more trouble. Watch memory usage to catch problems before they happen.

You can measure memory usage via the host resource MIB, or through the net-snmp MIB. Both provide details on memory usage. Different devices might support one, both, or neither, and to differing degrees. Some of that support is because of the nature of the device the agent is running on.

Both MIBs support measuring usage of physical memory, virtual memory, and swap space. You can easily use these objects to graph basic memory usage.

Both MIBs also offer insight into buffers and cache and other details of memory usage. You've probably seen these used to generate pretty graphs of exactly how a host's memory is utilized. These objects don't work on every agent, however, or might provide incomplete insight into the host's memory. If a Unix has multiple kinds of cache memory, the cache memory object might reflect only one of those caches. Add up the numbers reported by your agent and see if they seem to match reality. Often, you'll find AgentX modules that can extract that additional memory information for you.

Also verify the numbers reported by SNMP against what your host reports. If a host has 4GB of RAM and 2 GB of swap, it should have 6 GB of virtual memory. If the virtual memory object reports that the host has 2 GB of virtual memory, and its utilization mirrors that of swap space, this OID is only reporting swap usage. File a bug report with your Unix vendor.

If one MIB gives erroneous information, try the other MIB.

What a device reports depends on its operating system and its architecture. A router usually doesn't have swap space, so it's not going to report virtual memory statistics; all it has is physical RAM. It probably won't have any sort of buffer or cache. You'll see the device's total memory and memory used, because that's all the host has.

What's the difference between the two MIBs? The net-snmp MIB is easier to use. The host resource MIB is more likely to work.

Host Resource MIB Memory

If memory and swap appear in your agent's `hrStorageTable`, you can track and alarm on them. If you don't want to sort through the whole table, get an easy view of what different memory types an agent can provide about a particular host by walking `HOST-RESOURC-ES-MIB::hrStorageDescr`. Memory always appears first in this list.

```
$ snmpbulkwalk appserver1 hrStorageDescr
HOST-RESOURCES-MIB::hrStorageDescr.1 = STRING: Physical memory
HOST-RESOURCES-MIB::hrStorageDescr.2 = STRING: Real memory
HOST-RESOURCES-MIB::hrStorageDescr.3 = STRING: Virtual memory
HOST-RESOURCES-MIB::hrStorageDescr.6 = STRING: Memory buffers
HOST-RESOURCES-MIB::hrStorageDescr.7 = STRING: Cached memory
HOST-RESOURCES-MIB::hrStorageDescr.8 = STRING: Shared virtual memory
HOST-RESOURCES-MIB::hrStorageDescr.9 = STRING: Shared real memory
HOST-RESOURCES-MIB::hrStorageDescr.10 = STRING: Swap space
HOST-RESOURCES-MIB::hrStorageDescr.11 = STRING: swap ada0p2
HOST-RESOURCES-MIB::hrStorageDescr.35 = STRING: /
HOST-RESOURCES-MIB::hrStorageDescr.36 = STRING: /dev
...
```

The first line (index 1) shows *physical memory* or RAM. The first line shows us that we can track and alarm on memory.

The second line (index 2) shows real memory in use, or physical RAM used for applications.

The third line (index 3) shows virtual memory, which should be the combined physical RAM and swap space on the host.

Lines four and five (index 6 and 7) report buffer and cache memory.

Shared memory, on lines 6 and 7 (index 8 and 9) is memory that multiple processes access. If you're running twelve PHP processes, they don't all need their own in-memory copy of the PHP binary.

Finally, line 8 (index 10) gives the amount of swap space on the host.

Line 9 (index 11) is a particular swap partition. It mirrors line 8.

The list then devolves into partitions, which we don't care about right now.

Pick the indexes of the numbers you're interested in. The hr-StorageSize object gives the size of that memory device: the amount of RAM, or the amount of swap. Get the amount used from hrStorageUsed. You might want to alarm on hrStorageAllocationFailures to see if the host runs out of memory.

For example, you almost certainly want to track physical memory use. In our list above, it's index number 1. Get the size with HOST-RESOURCES-MIB::hrStorageSize.1 and monitor the amount in use with HOST-RESOURCES-MIB::hrStorageUsed.1.

Net-SNMP MIB Memory

Net-snmp provides a memory group in its enterprise MIB.

```
$ snmpbulkwalk www memory
UCD-SNMP-MIB::memIndex.0 = INTEGER: 0
UCD-SNMP-MIB::memErrorName.0 = STRING: swap
UCD-SNMP-MIB::memTotalSwap.0 = INTEGER: 2097024 kB
UCD-SNMP-MIB::memAvailSwap.0 = INTEGER: 1744932 kB
UCD-SNMP-MIB::memTotalReal.0 = INTEGER: 8349148 kB
UCD-SNMP-MIB::memAvailReal.0 = INTEGER: 216032 kB
UCD-SNMP-MIB::memTotalFree.0 = INTEGER: 102524 kB
UCD-SNMP-MIB::memMinimumSwap.0 = INTEGER: 16000 kB
UCD-SNMP-MIB::memShared.0 = INTEGER: 112540 kB
UCD-SNMP-MIB::memBuffer.0 = INTEGER: 0 kB
UCD-SNMP-MIB::memCached.0 = INTEGER: 262804 kB
UCD-SNMP-MIB::memSwapError.0 = INTEGER: noError(0)
UCD-SNMP-MIB::memSwapErrorMsg.0 = STRING:
```

The MIB declares that the first two objects, memIndex.0 and memErrorName.0, are bogus[37] and should be ignored.

---

37   This is not me being snarky. The definitions include the word "bogus." We need more standards with this degree of self-awareness.

Measure swap space with `memTotalSwap.0` (the amount of swap configured on the host) and `memAvailSwap.0` (the free swap space).

The `memTotalReal.0` OID gives the physical RAM on the host.

The OID `memAvailReal.0` has a deceiving name and is not to be trusted. It has nothing to do with available memory, but rather shows the amount of memory used by text pages. If the Unix differentiates text pages from other pages, that is. It is being deprecated in favor of a more accurately named object, `memUsedRealTXT`, so don't let this OID fool you.

To track available memory, use `memTotalFree.0`.

The `memShared.0`, `memBuffer.0`, and `memCached.0` OIDs show the amount of shared, buffer, and cache memory. As discussed earlier, these might or might not be relevant on your Unix.

Swap Use Alarms

Swap is meant to be used. Minor swap use is a sign of a healthy system. Most programs spend 90% of their time running 10% of their code, and those loaded but unneeded pages of program can be shuffled off to swap without penalty. A host should use its physical memory to perform real work. A small degree of paging is perfectly healthy. A host that starts to run low on swap space is in real trouble, though.

Net-snmp includes a feature to alarm when swap utilization goes above a certain point. The swap *snmpd.conf* keyword lets you set a minimum amount of free swap space. Give the minimum amount of free swap space, in kilobytes, as an argument. Here, I want an alarm when the free swap falls below 200 MB.

```
swap 204800
```

If swap drops below that amount, the OID `memSwapError.0` gets set to 1 and `memSwapErrorMsg.0` tells you how much swap remains.

Load Average Monitoring

The usefulness of load average is hotly debated. Every Unix calculates load average differently, so it's not a universal standard. Even on the same Unix, some applications run just fine with a load average of 20, while others choke and die at 2. Load average is only useful on a case-by-case basis. If you have that case, though, net-snmp lets you set alarms on load average.

Viewing Load Averages

View load information through the table `laTable`. Run `snmptable` ***hostname*** `laTable` and follow along.

The `laNames` column shows which load average the row represents. Load average is calculated in one-minute, five-minute, and fifteen-minute variants.

The `laLoad` column shows the current load average for each time window.

Under `laConfig` we see the load level that will cause an alarm. The default level is 12, for all three time periods. We'll override this later.

The `laLoadInt` column shows the current load in percent, as integers, while `laLoadFloat` gives it as a six-digit floating point.

The last two columns show the alarms. `laErrorFlag` is normally `noError`, but flips to `error` if the load gets too high. `laErrMessage` displays the problem, generally that the load average is unbearably high.

Setting Load Average Alarms

Use the *load* *snmpd.conf* keyword to configure load average alarms. It requires one, two, or three integer arguments, setting new maximum tolerable one-minute, five-minute, and fifteen-minute load averages.

```
load 1-minute 5-minute 15-minute
```

You don't have to define all three limits. If you define one or two limits, all remaining limits are set to the last defined limit. Here I set all three limits to 10.

```
load 10
```

Below I tolerate occasional peak loads, just in case my manager queries at a bad instant. If the 5-minute or 15-minute load exceeds 5, though, I want an alarm. I don't explicitly define a 15-minute load, so it uses the last configured value.

```
load 15 5
```

After much observation many false alarms, and a few cases where I should have been alarmed but wasn't, I've determined the proper limits for all three loads on my host.

```
load 15 5 4
```

Most often, I don't alarm on load average. I will graph it, however. Load average is a not-terrible way to evaluate how an individual system's workload evolves over time. It answers questions like "Is the server running slower since we patched it?" You can't measure "slowness," but load average is fair stand-in for "busyness."

Other Monitoring

This is only a taste of what SNMP lets you monitor. Run complete snmpbulkwalks against your agents and study the output. Look up the definitions of intriguing OIDs. Read articles and blogs about monitoring your equipment. If you want to make an extreme and sanity-risking effort, try the vendor documentation.

Net-snmp's agent has additional monitoring features that I don't discuss. It can monitor log file size, and even search log files for keywords. You can hard-code interface speed on troublesome device drivers, and define commands to fix errant processes when they error out. It can actively alarm on system changes. Modern management systems have better solutions for these problems today, but if you need the features in your agent they're there.

But what's in this chapter should keep you busy for quite some time. Let's turn the whole thing around now, and let agents speak to the manager.

Chapter 12: Notifications

Traditionally, an SNMP agent sits there passively twiddling its innumerable thumbs until a manager gives it a command. SNMP *traps, informs,* and *notifications* turn that around, allowing an agent, program, or device to send a message to a manager. Many embedded devices use traps to send events to a central host, such as UPSs that signal when they're on battery. Many network management systems include support for processing and alerting on SNMP notifications.

Before configuring notifications, consider if you need them. What mechanisms does your organization have for collecting and analyzing events? Can devices provide information via traps that is not already available by those other means? The answer depends entirely on your organization and your technology. Assuming you'd find traps useful, read on.

An SNMP *trap collector* or *trap receiver* is a daemon that listens for incoming SNMP notifications, both traps and informs. It can run on a different host than the regular SNMP manager, and doesn't necessarily need snmpd to function. I'll refer to these programs as *collectors* for brevity. We'll focus on the net-snmp trap collector, snmptrapd(8), but the general collector concepts apply to all collectors.

SNMPv1 traps are written in SMI-1, while SNMPv2c and SNMPv3 traps use SMI-2. The trap components are pretty similar, but the newer format is simpler and easier to use. Collectors that can accept SNMPv2c/SNMPv3 traps can most often accept SNMPv1 traps. When we send traps for testing we will use the newer format, and you should use that format for anything you implement.

Many embedded systems that don't have SNMP agents can emit SNMP notifications. Few of these speak SNMPv3; often you're lucky to get SNMPv2c. Even if your whole network is otherwise SNMPv3, you'll have to cope with SNMPv1 and SNMPv2c notifications. The universe is full of poorly-documented helpless little devices that can barely whimper for aid, and you'll need the capability to do something reasonable with those alerts. If one of these devices gives you trouble, break out a packet sniffer and see what they're really sending.

It is possible, though unwieldy, to interpret standard notifications manually. After a little practice you'll recognize "the router says interface 12 flapped" and "someone restarted snmpd." Complicated enterprise notifications with dozens of objects will quickly melt your brain, however. You'll want a network management system like OpenNMS to perform such labor for you. If you have no plans to implement such a system, trap collection is pretty much a complicated logging exercise.[38] Logging verifies you're receiving the notifications, though. It's a start.

Collecting notifications requires deciding on what SNMP commands you will support, picking the authentication and privacy options, and figuring out what you'll do with the traps you receive.

Trap Operations

What we call "traps" includes two different SNMP commands, TRAP and INFORM. They're generally lumped together as *notifications*, although many people call both sorts "traps."

An SNMP TRAP operation is the original agent-to-manager message. It is the only notification supported by SNMPv1. The message gets flung across the network to the manager with no verification or acknowledgement. A TRAP uses a community or SNMPv3 user for authentication. It's much like syslog plus a dash of authentication.

An INFORM operation includes both the agent sending the manager a message, and the manager acknowledging the message. An agent that doesn't receive a receipt for an INFORM will retransmit the INFORM until it receives an acknowledgement or its vendor-dependent timeout lapses. SNMPv2c and SNMPv3 support INFORM. INFORM operations authenticate via communities or SNMPv3 users.

---

38   There's no feeling quite like doing a post-mortem on a twelve hour outage, only to read the logs and discover that the problem router was begging for help for the last month.

I recommend using INFORM for your notifications whenever possible. Not only do acknowledgements make INFORM a distinct improvement over logging protocols like syslog, in SNMPv3 configuring a TRAP user is more complicated than an INFORM user. If you have a lot of equipment, however, load might become a problem. You might need to fall back to TRAP and maintain engine IDs in your user accounts, or even revert certain notifications to SNMPv2c.

The Trap Collector: snmptrapd(8)

Net-snmp includes a notification collector, snmptrapd(8). It uses the same configuration file style as the other net-snmp programs, including the wide variety of possible file locations and the ability to suck in configuration values from other net-snmp programs. I recommend putting `snmptrapd.conf` right next to your other system-wide configuration files, in either `/etc/snmp/` or `/usr/local/etc/`, and configuring everything in that one file.

There's also a persistent data file, where snmptrapd stores notification-specific information. Back up this file regularly. As with the persistent `snmpd.conf` file, losing the persistent `snmptrapd.conf` will force you to recreate all of your notification user accounts.

Communicating with snmptrapd

You can run snmptrapd with an empty configuration file. It won't collect any notifications, but it will start. Enable and run it. If you watch your system logs, you'll see snmptrapd connect to the local snmpd agent via AgentX. It doesn't register any additional objects with the agent, however. You can communicate with snmptrapd, but only on its own terms.

Snmptrapd uses an SNMP *context*. We discussed context briefly in Chapter 1, and said it was something you rarely needed. This is the rarity. By specifying a context in your SNMP command line, you can tell snmpd "Patch me through to this other thing." Use −n to give the context name. Here, I interrogate snmptrapd via snmpbulkwalk, using the context name "snmptrapd."

```
$ snmpbulkwalk -n snmptrapd appserver1 .1
NOTIFICATION-LOG-MIB::nlmConfigGlobalEntryLimit.0 =
    Gauge32: 1000
NOTIFICATION-LOG-MIB::nlmConfigGlobalAgeOut.0 =
    Gauge32: 1440 minutes
NOTIFICATION-LOG-MIB::nlmStatsGlobalNotificationsLogged.0 =
    Counter32: 0 notifications
NOTIFICATION-LOG-MIB::nlmStatsGlobalNotificationsBumped.0 =
    Counter32: 0 notifications
...
```

This brand-new collector has 11 objects, all for collection statistics, and all the counters are at zero. It hasn't done anything yet. All of our usual snmp commands work on snmptrapd, so long as you specify the context. You must use snmpd users, not the users we'll configure later for snmptrapd.

Monitoring snmptrapd

As long as you're monitoring everything else, you might as well monitor snmptrapd as well.

The table `nlmLogTable` lists received notifications. It includes OIDs and multiple engine IDs, so it's quite wide no matter what you do, but it's worth looking at. The table contains a maximum of 1000 entries, but you can adjust this by setting `nlmConfigGlobalEntryLimit.0`. Entries age out after `nlmConfigGlobalAgeOut.0` minutes.

The object `nlmStatsGlobalNotificationsLogged.0` shows how many notifications have been put in the log table. It's not the current size of the log table, but how many entries have been added to the table since snmptrapd was last restarted. A sudden spike in notifications merits investigation.

So far, all of these objects are empty. Let's fill them with notifications.

Notifications

Notifications are SNMP objects. They're defined in MIB files amidst all the other objects, they are assigned an OID, and must conform to the narrow definitions set by the MIB. A notification definition declares what the notification represents and valid values it can take. Many notifications piggyback on objects you use for monitoring.

Notification Types

SNMP defines six standard notifications, but one (EGP neighbor loss) is obsolete. Not all agents can send all of these notifications, and you don't have to configure all notifications in your agents. You can also use custom notifications, but we'll start with the classics.

The *warmStart* notification (`SNMPv2-MIB::warmStart`) is used for when an agent is resetting itself but its configuration should remain unchanged. You could think of this as a SIGHUP notification. Very few agents use this, however.

The *coldStart* notification (`SNMPv2-MIB::coldStart`) is used for when a device or application is starting up from nothing. The configuration of the device or service could have changed from the last time it was running. You can see this when you reboot a router or restart `snmpd`.

The *linkDown* (`IF-MIB::linkDown`) and *linkUp* (`IF-MIB-::linkUp`) notifications indicate that a network interface has gone down or up. Interfaces are numbered by their index in `ifXTable`. You'll see entries like `linkUp.5` and `linkDown.89`.

The last standard notification, *authenticationFailure* (`SN-MPv2-MIB::authenticationFailure`), fires when someone tries to authenticate to a device or application, but fails. Applications might send this notification whenever an unknown user tries to log in, or only when a known user fails to authenticate.

Organizations can also define their own notifications in their MIBs. So long as you have the appropriate MIB files, you can interpret

231

those. We'll start with the standard ones, but play with some custom notifications as well.

Notification Components

All notifications have a few elements in common. Every notification includes the sending agent's uptime, for a start.

All notifications include the OID `SNMPv2-MIB::sn-mpTrapOID.0`, often called snmpTrapOID. This object describes how the collector should process the notification, and is most often related to the notification type. If you're sending a `linkUp` notification, snmpTrapOID would be `IF-MIB::linkUp`. If you're sending a vendor notification, snmpTrapOID would be something from the vendor's MIB file. Snmptrapd can selectively process and filter notifications based on snmpTrapOID.

Other information comes along as variable bindings, or *varbinds*. A varbind is a group of three pieces of information: an OID, a data type, and a value, much like a SET command (Chapter 7). If an interface goes down, the agent might assemble a varbind like "the oid for this interface's status, type integer, is 2." Your monitoring system assembles varbinds into notifications, which it sends to the collector. The collector disassembles the notification into varbinds, picks the varbinds apart, and interprets them. It probably sends you a message like "this interface on this host went down," which you promptly ignore.

Notification Authentication

Net-snmp's trap collector users have no relationship to those in the agent. Other vendors might combine those databases, or have pointy-clicky interfaces where you can assign certain users to specific roles. We're going to talk net-snmp here.

Any users or communities configured in your agent or manager are irrelevant to SNMP notifications. Additionally, SNMPv3 users for TRAP and INFORM operations have slightly different requirements.

Configure all user and community access in `snmptrapd.conf`. Much as with snmpd, you must set up SNMPv3 users elsewhere before you can grant them access.

SNMPv3 Users

You manage snmptrapd users much like snmpd users. While net-snmp includes the net-snmp-create-v3-user(1) command to ease setting up a bootstrap user in snmpd, there's no such tool for snmptrapd. You must configure your bootstrap user manually. Users who can send a TRAP must always be created by hand. There's a couple of ways to do this, and they're both kind of annoying.

You can create template users in the standard `snmptrapd.conf`. The advantage of this is that you can change the configuration while the trap collector is running. The disadvantage is that the user creation statements includes the user's authentication credentials in plain text. Anyone with permission to view the file can see the new user's passphrases. Once you restart snmptrapd and the daemon creates the user accounts in the persistent data file, you must edit the configuration file again to remove the accounts. I would advise restarting snmptrapd one more time to verify that your simple harmless edit didn't break snmptrapd.

Alternately, you can create users directly in the persistent data file. The configuration to do so is exactly like that used in the standard configuration file. As snmptrapd rewrites this file every time it gets signaled to do so, restarts, or stops, you can only edit this file when snmptrapd is not running. The user creation command will remain as plain text in the file the first time you start snmptrapd. After the next restart, they'll get replaced by the usual hashed-up user account entries. The good news is, unprivileged users cannot view the persistent data file.

Which should you use? That depends entirely on your threat model. My gut insists that if you routinely edit the persistent data file Nodens will hunt down your user database and fling it off the edge of dreamland, but you might prefer that over having passphrases temporarily visible to other sysadmins. Choose your own doom.

You can view all snmptrapd users with snmptable(1) by specifying the *snmptrapd* context.

```
$ snmptable -n snmptrapd -Cb appserver1 usmUserTable
```

Similarly, once you have a bootstrap snmptrapd user, you can clone that user to add new snmptrapd users.

As with standard SNMPv3 users, each account needs encryption methods and passphrases of eight characters or more.

SNMPv3 INFORM Users

Use the *createUser* keyword in `snmptrapd.conf` to create INFORM users. You must specify the encryption authentication and privacy algorithms and the passphrase for each.

```
createUser username auth-alg auth-passphrase \
     privacy-alg privacy-passphrase
```

Here I create a user **informUser**. It uses SHA-256 for authentication and AES128 for privacy. The authentication passphrase is *seekrit1*, while the privacy passphrase is *s3kr3t22*.

```
createUser informUser SHA-256 seekrit1 AES128 s3kr3t22
```

Add this entry to `snmptrapd.conf` and restart the daemon.

You must also grant the user access in `snmptrapd.conf`, as we'll see later.

SNMPv3 TRAP Users

A user account for sending a TRAP *must* include the engine ID of the host that's sending the trap.[39] Every agent that supports SNMPv3 makes its engine ID available at `SNMP-FRAMEWORK-MIB::snmpEngineID.0`.

---

39   The reasons for this make perfect sense once you study the SNMP standard in sufficient detail, but such all-encompassing comprehension also means that every time you look at another human being you'll tumble through their skull into the universe within, so I can't recommend it.

```
$ snmpget router1 SNMP-FRAMEWORK-MIB::snmpEngineID.0
SNMP-FRAMEWORK-MIB::snmpEngineID.0 =
        Hex-STRING: 80 00 1F 88 80 E0 BD A7 65 66 9C 93...
```

You'll use the −e flag and this hex number (without spaces) as an argument to *createUser* in `snmptrapd.conf`. Here I create a TRAP user, **router1Trap**, that uses the same authentication settings as the IN-FORM user.

```
createUser -e 0x80001F8880E0BDA765669C935D000000 \
        router1Trap SHA-256 seekrit3 AES128 s3kr3t44
```

This user can only be used from an agent with the given engineID. Yes, this means that every SNMPv3 agent that sends TRAP must have a unique user account. Some agents will change their engine ID, which means you must update the account used to send TRAPs. Additionally, while you can change a user's passphrases with snmpusm, you cannot change or view the user's engine ID that way.

If you want to share a notification account across multiple agents, and withstand agents changing their engine ID under arbitrary circumstances, verify that your SNMPv3 "traps" are really INFORMs.

Testing Notification Users

TRAP and INFORM users are obscured from the usual management tools. If the user doesn't work, though, nothing else will. Simultaneously debugging user accounts and the collector is infuriating. Verify that the account works before proceeding. The collector doesn't respond to queries the way an agent does, so you can't just run snmpstatus(1) to verify connectivity. By the time you get this far in this book, fortunately, you know more about SNMP than is good for your mental health. We can get creative.

We're going to run snmptrapd in the foreground with −f, and direct all its output to standard out with −Lo. The −D flag enables debugging. The debug flag needs a module name as an argument. Users are in the usm module. Finally, we can't run multiple collectors on the same port. Run this collector on UDP port 163.

```
# snmptrapd -f -Lo -Dusm udp:163
```

The daemon will show a little annoyance at running on an off port, but it will settle down with a banner declaring the net-snmp version and wait for someone to authenticate to it.

Go to another terminal window, even one on the same host. We'll use snmpstatus to query the collector. It won't return an answer, but it will attempt to authenticate. We can watch the authentication in the snmptrapd session. We ran snmpstatus in Chapter 2, back when we still had hope. Use -v 3 to give the SNMP version, and -l to specify a security level. The -u provides the username. Give the authentication algorithm and passphrase with -a and -A, and the privacy algorithm and passphrase with -x and -X. Lastly, you need a target host and a port. Here I'm using the **informUser** account we just configured. I'm sending the request to the host **traphost** on port 163.

```
$ snmpstatus -v3 -l priv -u informUser -a SHA-256 \
    -A seekrit1 -x AES128 -X s3kr3t22 traphost:163
```

The terminal window will hang for a few seconds, as snmpstatus attempts to evoke a response from the collector. Over in the running snmptrapd session, though, you'll see messages like this.

```
...
usm: USM processing begun...
usm: Unknown Engine ID.
usm: USM processing has begun (offset 56)
usm: getting user
usm: USM processing completed.
usm: USM processing begun...
usm: match on user informUser
...
```

The "Unknown Engine ID" message is an artifact of us using snmpstatus on a program that doesn't support its queries. You'll see a few lines of the USM module chewing the authentication request. If it spits out a "match on user" message for your username, you authenticated successfully. If the user isn't known, or your authentication passphrase is wrong, snmpstatus will tell you.

Test your trap user the same way. You must add one more flag, -e for the engine ID.

```
$ snmpstatus -e 0x80001f8880e0bda765669c935d000000 \
    -v3 -l priv -u router1Trap -a SHA-256 -A seekrit1 \
    -x AES128 -X s3kr3t22 traphost:163
```

Exit the debugging session. Be sure to copy the command line you used to successfully authenticate to the collector. Folks very rarely send traps at the command line, so there's no convenient configuration file option for these settings, and you *will* need them.

Collector Access Rules

Once you have functional user accounts, grant them collector access in `snmptrapd.conf`. User access rules have this general format.

```
authUser privileges username <security level> OID
```

The collector has three possible privileges: log, execute, and net. The *log* privilege lets messages from this account be logged to syslogd. The *execute* privilege lets messages from this account be handed off to an external processing script. The *net* privilege lets messages from this account be forwarded to another collector. These actions aren't requested by external users; rather, rules later in `snmptrapd.conf` will process notifications based on these privileges.

The username is the user you configured outside of snmptrapd.

The security level is one of *noauth*, *auth*, or *priv*. If you don't specify a security level , it defaults to *auth*.

You can optionally add permitted OIDs to the end of a user entry, but the collector only compares the contents of `snmpTrapOID` to your list. This makes such restrictions largely ineffective.

Here I grant messages from **informUser** complete access to the collector, so long as they use *priv* security.

```
authUser log,execute,net informUser priv
```

If you've been sentenced to older SNMP versions, configure communities with the *authCommunity* keyword.

```
authCommunity privileges username OID
```

Here I grant the community **informCommunity** execute and log access to the collector.

```
authCommunity log,execute informCommunity
```

Restart snmptrapd. You should now be able to send notifications to the collector.

Running snmptrapd

We now have an *snmptrapd.conf* with a couple of user rules in it. You can now enable and run snmptrapd.

```
# service snmptrapd start
```

If you start the collector now, it will log all traps received to syslog using the daemon facility. This dumps your SNMP notifications in amidst the rest of the system logs. I recommend using a dedicated syslog facility by setting –Ls and a facility on the snmptrapd command line, as discussed in Chapter 6. Here I run snmptrapd to log to facility local7. I'd still need to configure my local logging server, whatever it is, to send local7 messages to a file like */var/log/trap*.

```
# snmptrapd -Ls 7
```

The rest of this chapter assumes that you send all of your traps to */var/log/trap*.

Your First Notification: snmpd(8)

The simplest way to send notifications is from the local agent. Snmpd will send notifications when it shuts down, when it starts, and when a known user gives incorrect authentication information. As you can restart snmpd more easily than you can unplug cables from a router, it's the most controllable source of notifications.

Configure notifications with the *trapsess* `snmpd.conf` keyword. Remember when I had you record the command lines used to verify your SNMPv3 accounts? You'll need them here. The *trapsess* keyword contains the command line arguments needed to successfully communicate with your collector. All those arguments you needed on your snmpstatus command go right here. Put a `-Ci` at the front, to tell `snmpd` to send an INFORM rather than a TRAP.

```
trapsess -Ci -v3 -l priv -u informUser -a SHA-256 \
     -A seekrit1 -x AES128 -X s3kr3t22 traphost
```

If you want a notification any time a known user fails to send the correct authentication information, you can set the *authtrapenable* keyword to 1.

```
authtrapenable 1
```

Restart snmpd, and check `/var/log/trap`. The log will give you a hint about what you did wrong.

```
Dec 11 18:08:35 traphost snmptrapd[10342]:
     Authentication failed for informUser
```

If by some unlikely chance you did everything correctly, you will see your first SNMP notifications.

```
Dec 11 17:34:44 traphost snmptrapd[10342]:
  2019-12-11 17:34:44 crawlingchaos.mwl.io [UDP:
  [203.0.113.206]:44969->[203.0.113.207]:162]:
  DISMAN-EVENT-MIB::sysUpTimeInstance = Timeticks:
  (11) 0:00:00.11       SNMPv2-MIB::snmpTrapOID.0 = OID:
  SNMPv2-MIB::coldStart SNMPv2-MIB::snmpTrapEnterprise.0
  = OID: NET-SNMP-MIB::netSnmpAgentOIDs.10
```

You caught a thing! It might even mean something.

Interpreting Traps

Let's dissect that first notification.

```
Dec 11 17:34:44 traphost snmptrapd[10342]:
```

This message was received on the host **traphost**, from a local **snmptrapd** process. Everything that follows is the SNMP notification.

```
2019-12-11 17:34:44 crawlingchaos.mwl.io [UDP:
[203.0.113.206]:44969->[203.0.113.207]:162]:
```

This message was received on 11 December 2019, at 5:34:44 PM. It came from the host **crawlingchaos.mwl.io**. We get the source and destination IP address and port.

```
DISMAN-EVENT-MIB::sysUpTimeInstance =
      Timeticks: (11) 0:00:00.11
```

The notification included the OID `DISMAN-EVENT-MIB::sy-sUpTimeInstance`. It was set to 11. This is the agent uptime, and is included in all notifications.

```
SNMPv2-MIB::snmpTrapOID.0 = OID: SNMPv2-MIB::coldStart
```

Here we have the snmpTrapOID, required in every SNMP notification. This notification contains the object `SNMPv2-MIB::cold-Start`. It's a coldStart message, indicating that the agent was started (or restarted).

```
SNMPv2-MIB::snmpTrapEnterprise.0 =
      OID: NET-SNMP-MIB::netSnmpAgentOIDs.10
```

An snmptranslate run tells me that `SNMPv2-MIB::sn-mpTrapEnterprise.0` is "the authoritative identification of the enterprise associated with the trap." Further reading shows that it appears at the end of any notification that is translated from the SNMPv1 to SNMPv2c/SNMPv3 format. We can guess that the net-snmp agent sends notifications formatted in the SNMPv1 style. The value of this object tells us that this notification was created by a net-snmp agent.

You can change the format of these log messages. See the *format* keyword in *snmptrapd.conf*(5) and the format character definitions in snmptrapd(8).

Congratulations. You have a working collector.

Sending Notifications by Hand

More complex notifications merit special processing. Maybe you want certain notifications sent via email, others pumped into a database, and still others filed under /dev/null. You can write external handlers for most of these functions. Writing such a script means you must be able to run the script whenever required. This means you need the power to generate notifications on demand. You can do so with snmptrap(1) and snmpinform(1).

A notification must comply with its MIB, even when you generate it manually. Programs like snmpinform will not accept a syntactically invalid message. The easiest way to get such syntax is to capture it from the log file. If the right kind of notification hasn't been generated yet, though, you're stuck delving into the MIB.[40] We're going to use the netSnmpExampleHeartbeatNotification OID from NET-SNMP-EXAMPLES-MIB as an example. According to the MIB it includes a mandatory OID, netSnmpExampleHeartbe- atRate, of type integer. There's also an optional OID, netSnmpEx- ampleHeartbeatName, of type string. I'm going to send both of these to my collector.

Run snmpinform like so.

```
$ snmpinform <connectinfo> sysUptime snmpTrapOid \
    notification
```

The connection information includes all of the options needed to find your collector and authenticate to it. For our example user, this would be -v3 -l priv -u informUser -a SHA-256 -A seekrit1 -x AES128 -X s3kr3t22 traphost.

Every notification must include how long the system or agent has been running. The snmpinform command knows you must include this, but you also need the option to override the true value. If you en-

---

40   Or contacting the vendor. I suspect that's an even faster path to madness, however.

ter "" for the uptime, it will use the correct agent uptime. You can enter an integer here, if your brain measures time more accurately than a computer.

The snmpTrapOid contains the OID of the notification object. The full formal OID of our notification is `NET-SNMP-EXAMPLES-MIB-::netSnmpExampleHeartbeatNotification`.

We now have two objects to set within this notification. Each object is a varbind, so it much include the OID, the type, and the value. The OID `netSnmpExampleHeartbeatRate` is an integer, type `i`. I'll set it to 13524. `netSnmpExampleHeartbeatName` is a string, type `s`. I'll give the heartbeat a name.

Putting all this together, we get:

```
$ snmpinform -v3 -l priv -u informUser -a SHA-256 \
  -A seekritl -x AES128 -X s3kr3t22 traphost "" \
  NET-SNMP-EXAMPLES-MIB::netSnmpExampleHeartbeatNotification \
  netSnmpExampleHeartbeatRate i 13524 \
  netSnmpExampleHeartbeatName s Nyarlathotep
```

If you're debugging a script, you can fortunately just hammer the up arrow. So, let's talk about scripts and notification routing.

Notification Processing

Presumably, you set up notifications because you want to do something with them. Snmptrapd lets you select notifications for special handling, or set default handling, in *trap handlers*. or *notification handlers*. You can select notifications by the OID given in the notification's snmpTrapOid. In addition to logging notifications, snmptrapd can forward them or route them through scripts.

Forwarding Notifications

The simplest processing is forwarding the notification to another collector, with the *forward* keyword.

```
forward OID collector
```

The OID can appear either by name, or numerically.

The collector can be the hostname or IP address of the collector. The formats used to set snmpd or snmptrapd listening address can be used to adjust protocol or port.

Here, I forward all of the standard network interface notifications to the network team's collector on the host **networkarchive**. The collector runs on port 999, and we need to use TCP because UDP makes the firewall administrator even more twitchy.

```
forward IF-MIB::linkDown  tcp:networkarchive:999
forward IF-MIB::linkUp    tcp:networkarchive:999
```

You can use numerical OIDs and a wildcard to capture everything at or below a certain OID. Here, I send everything from a particular vendor to the collector on host **unspeakable**.

```
forward .1.3.6.1.4.1.9* unspeakable
```

If the OID has a period before the wildcard (.1.3.6.1.4.1.9.*), it captures everything below the OID but not the OID itself.

You can use the OID default to catch any notifications that are not forwarded by more specific *forward* statements. The security team wants a copy of all notifications that don't already get routed somewhere sent forwarded to their team at the host **auditcollector**.

```
forward default auditcollector
```

I do not envy anyone the job of auditing all unknown SNMP notifications.

Notification Scripts

You can forward any notification to an external script. The most common use for this is to feed SNMP notifications to external software such as Icinga or Nagios. These systems all provide instructions on how to get snmptrapd to feed them. Follow those instructions. Look at this information only for debugging.

If you want to write your own notification handler, you can do that. Be aware that snmptrapd will block and stop processing incoming notifications while your script runs. Your script must be extremely fast. Don't go making XMLRPC over HTTPS calls across the world, you'll miss a whole bunch of things.

Use the *traphandle* keyword to route notifications to a program. The syntax is exactly the same as the *forward* keyword, down to the wildcards and the catch-everything-else OID *default*. Here I forward all of the standard coldStart notifications to the script `/scripts/restarted.sh`. The script gets run with one argument, *trouble*.

```
traphandle SNMPv2-MIB::coldStart /scripts/restarted.sh trouble
```

The script receives the notification on standard input. The hostname comes first, then the connection information, each on their own line. Each OIDs and its value follows, each pair on its own line.

That manual notification we sent in the last section? Let's send it to a script. When `netSnmpExampleHeartbeatNotification` arrives, we'll route it to `/scripts/pulse.sh`. Presumably, we set up a handler for this particular object because we need to run the handler script with specific arguments. I'm setting this to use the arguments this script needs for this particular trap, *five phase heartbeat*.

```
traphandle \
NET-SNMP-EXAMPLES-MIB::netSnmpExampleHeartbeatNotification \
/scripts/pulse.sh five phase heartbeat
```

Here's a sample script. It logs the contents of each notification to the file `/tmp/pulse`. Such a script can be useful to verify what snmptrapd is passing to your external program. If your script isn't behaving, try something like this to validate that the objects and values you're receiving are what you think they are.

```
#!/bin/sh
read host
read ip

(
   echo "=====new trap====="
   echo "arguments are: $*"
   echo "host is: $host"
   echo "connection is: $ip"
   echo "OIDs are:"
   while read oid val
   do
      echo "$oid = $val"
   done
   echo '-----END OF TRAP-----'
   echo ' '
) >> /tmp/pulse
```

You can change the information snmptrapd sends to external scripts, just as you can reformat log messages. See the *format* keyword in snmptrapd.conf(5) and the format character definitions in snmptrapd(8).

Again, I strongly recommend not writing your own external handlers. If your life lacks trouble, I would suggest taking up cactus licking before digging into SNMP handlers. Sometimes, though, systems administration doesn't give us such pleasant options.

You now know more about SNMP than almost any other computing professional. I'm sorry. I'm so, so sorry.

Afterword

I wrote this book as a public service.

Many folks clam there are better options than SNMP. I've tried lots them. None are as flexible or omnipresent as SNMP. Every environment I've worked in, we've wound up falling back on SNMP for at least part of our infrastructure management. The fact that so few people understand it, and so many people loathe it, are joyful bonuses for those of us with an abhorrent sense of humor.

The whole Lovecraftian horror motif started as a throwaway joke, but suited the topic disturbingly well. The aspects of Lovecraft's character that compelled him to create cosmic horror, though, also hindered his work and ruined his life. Many people have taken his ideas and transcended them. I encourage you to check out the work of modern writers like Damien Angelica Walters, Victor LaValle, Caitlín R. Kiernan, Richard Thomas, Laird Barron, Helen Oyemi, Matt Huff, John Langan, Kristi DeMeester, Mary SanGiovanni, Brian Keene, and Lucy A. Snyder, who could all show Lovecraft how it's done.

And after spending months with SNMP, I can now see triangles with 270 degrees and colors that have no place on a wholesome spectrum. It's clearly time for a break, at least until the shoggoth stop scratching at my windows.

Patronizers

Certain fine folks send me money every month via Patreon. The folks here send me so much money, I agreed to put their names in the back of every book I write. Peter Wemm and Allan Jude, plus Daisy the Shepherdbane and Hellpuppy, all support me enough to get their names in the back of the ebooks. Phillip Vuchetich, Stefan Johnson, and Jeffrey David Marraccini support me so much, I must put their names in the back of both the ebook *and* print editions.

Additionally, I must single out Kate Ebneter for especial thanks. It's not enough that she was the First Wildebeest to drink from my print-level Patronizer pool, demonstrating it was safe for others to come in. I somehow completely faceplanted in crediting her when *Terrapin Sky Tango* first came out. She was completely sweet about my unfathomable incompetence.

Don't think she's a pushover, though. I'm told that if you say Kate's name five times fast in a mirror she will appear, riding that First Wildebeest, and trample you before returning to the Home for People who are Too Good for this World.

Sponsors

These people wanted the book to exist so badly that they paid me to write it. They paid me so much that I'm putting their names here. It would be more appropriate to engrave their names on an ancient ruined obelisk on the Leng Plateau, but that would involve leaving the house and there's *people* out there. Some of these folks also appear on the Patronizer list. They need someone to take over their finances for them before they bankrupt themselves quixotically over-supporting us weird artistic types.

In all seriousness: thank you all. I spent more time wrangling MIB files and less worrying about the mortgage because of you.

Stefan Johnson

Adam Thompson

Michael Williams

Bob Eager

Rogier Krieger

Chris Dunbar

Trix Farrar

David Hansen

tanamar corporation

Dan Parriott

John W. O'Brien

Russell Folk

Florian Obser

Jan-Piet Mens

Trond Endrestøl

Nicholas Brenckle

Marcin Cieślak

Jason Dixon

Chris Hawkins

Kate Ebneter

Phi Network Systems

Joachim Ernst

Never miss a new Lucas release!

Sign up for Michael W Lucas' mailing lists.

https://mwl.io

www.ingramcontent.com/pod-product-compliance
Lightning Source LLC
LaVergne TN
LVHW050146060326
832904LV00019B/330/J